MINDFUL PARENTING HABITS

26 PRACTICES FOR RAISING YOUR CHILD WITH MORE PRESENCE AND LESS STRESS

(FROM INFANCY TO KINDERGARTEN)

BARRIE DAVENPORT

S.J. SCOTT

ISBN: 978-1-946159-22-9

DISCLAIMER

No part of this publication may be reproduced or transmitted in any form or by any means, mechanical or electronic, including photocopying or recording, or by any information storage and retrieval system, or transmitted by email without permission in writing from the publisher.

While all attempts have been made to verify the information provided in this publication, neither the author nor the publisher assumes any responsibility for errors, omissions, or contrary interpretations of the subject matter herein.

The views expressed in this book are those of the author alone, and should not be taken as expert instruction or commands. The reader is responsible for his or her own actions.

Adherence to all applicable laws and regulations, including international, federal, state, and local governing professional licensing, business practices, advertising, and all other aspects of doing business in the US, Canada, or any other jurisdiction is the sole responsibility of the purchaser or reader.

Neither the author nor the publisher assumes any responsibility or liability whatsoever on the behalf of the purchaser or reader of these materials.

Any perceived slight of any individual or organization is purely unintentional.

Contents

The Reality of Parenting

Parenting is one of the most challenging, demanding, and stressful jobs on the planet. It is also one of the most important, for how it is done influences in great measure the heart and soul and consciousness of the next generation.

— Jon and Myla Kabat-Zinn, *Everyday Blessings: The Inner Work of Mindful Parenting*

It's 3:45 a.m. and you can hear that telltale snuffling sound on the baby monitor that precedes a full-throated wail. Maybe he'll go back to sleep if you wait a few minutes. You close your eyes and start to drift off, but just as you do, the wailing begins.

You change him, feed him, rock him, walk him—and finally, a little after 5:00, he falls asleep. Maybe you can catch another hour or so of sleep before you have to get your first-grader up and on the bus then head to work. But at 5:30, there she is, standing at your bedside holding pungent pajama bottoms. "Mommy, I wet the bed."

Nothing prepares you for the huge difference between your vision of parenthood before you have children and the reality that smacks you in the face once they arrive.

Your dreams of peacefully sleeping babies who rarely cry, perfectly behaved toddlers who never have tantrums, and preternaturally gifted school children who excel at every endeavor rarely materialize.

The journey of parenthood is unpredictable and bumpy, often fraught with exhaustion, resentment, frustration, exasperation, disappointments, overwhelm, and boredom.

1

That's not to say there aren't plenty of rewarding and fulfilling times. There are. It's also not to say your heart doesn't overflow with love. It does. But as a cartoon we read recently asks, "Is it possible to love the child standing in front of you with all your heart and still want them to leave the room?" It definitely is.

You may wonder how you can manage the slings and arrows of parenthood and still cherish those sacred moments when your baby is sleeping like an angel, your toddler gives you wet kiss and says, "I love you Mommy," or your five-year-old stars as the turkey in the Thanksgiving play.

How can you remain present with your child, with yourself, and with the process of parenting through both the fulfilling and challenging times while maintaining your sanity and maybe even enjoying the process?

We believe the best way to be the kind of parent you want to be and fully embrace the joys and heartaches of parenthood is through *mindful parenting*—an approach that applies the practices of mindfulness to child-rearing, family life, and yourself.

Sounds simple enough, right?

The concept is simple. The application—not so much.

When your toddler throws herself on the floor in a kicking-and-screaming heap in the grocery store, and all eyes are on you, piercing your self-control with judgmental stares, mindfulness isn't the first thing that comes to mind.

Likewise, when you're going on five hours of sleep and still have many more hours of chores ahead of you before bed, sitting in the lotus position to meditate is laughable.

In the context of parenting, mindfulness rarely involves zoning out and seeking nirvana—although that might sound especially appealing when you're in the throes of parenting hell.

Mindful parenting is intentional, conscious, and attentive parenting in both good times and bad. It involves giving yourself the space and mental focus to be proactive rather than reactive, and to be thoughtful and compassionate in your interactions with your children, your spouse, and yourself.

It means knowing your priorities and allowing lesser things to fall away, even in the face of outside pressures or trends.

The life of a busy parent doesn't naturally lend itself to moments of inner contemplation or outer calm. There's enough drama and stress that occur in one day to trigger every emotional hot button you possess. Sometimes just getting through the day without killing someone feels like a win.

However, if you prioritize mindfulness as the centerpiece of your parenting and home-life efforts, you'll encounter a surprising shift in your mindset and emotional equilibrium.

As a mindful parent, you'll be prepared for better responses during these high-stress times and have more bandwidth to savor the joyful times. You'll also create an environment in which your children can practice mindful behaviors and make choices that will serve them throughout their lives.

Who Is This Book For?

If you're a parent of a child or children with ages between infancy and preschool, or if you are planning to have children, this book is written for you.

Whether life is going smoothly right now with your child (or children), you're facing the typical challenges inherent in your child's stage of development, or you have a particularly difficult situation (such as a special needs child), you'll find that the strategies we provide will support and enhance your parenting efforts.

We want to help you apply mindfulness as a parent in a variety of ways, such as:

- Determining the kind of parent you want to be.
- Working in tandem with your spouse or partner to be a team and present a unified front to your children.
- Being fully present with your children in difficult, neutral, and happy times.
- Learning new ways to respond during high-stress, challenging, tedious, and uncomfortable situations with your children.
- Being aware of your child's unique needs and personality so you can tailor your decisions, responses, and expectations accordingly.
- Creating an environment in your home that reinforces mindfulness.

- Evaluating your family priorities with more emphasis on simplicity and quality time and less on busyness and material things.

- Creating realistic schedules, activities, and rules that foster more presence and less distraction.

- Learning to be more mindful yourself so you have the space to be available to your children and family.

We'll state up front something you probably already know: You won't be a perfect parent. And you certainly won't be perfectly mindful all day, every day. That's impossible for anyone. Our goal isn't to add another unrealistic activity to your already hectic and demanding life.

Rather, it's to help you become *more aware* as a parent by learning some simple practices that are easy to apply to your daily life. The more you practice being mindful and making mindful choices, the more you will reap the rewards of a calmer, happier, and more bonded family life. In fact, just a little mindfulness in parenting goes a long way.

- When you step back in the heat of the moment, observe your emotions, and consider your response, you are being more mindful.

- When you listen to your child for a few minutes without looking at your phone or letting your mind wander, you are being more mindful.

- When you decide that your child doesn't really need the extra Saturday morning swim lesson (even though all of your friends' kids are participating), you are being more mindful.

- When you stop to recognize that your child's anger isn't just defiance, but rather fear or insecurity, you are being more mindful.

All of these small choices and actions add up and help you and your child become more confident and secure in yourselves, your roles, and your lives together. They create an atmosphere that is less stressful and more tuned-in to the deeper needs of each member of the family.

Will mindfulness stop your head from spinning off when your child acts up or when you're exhausted? Not always. But it will help you temper your responses or come back to your child later with a better, more attentive response.

Will mindfulness ensure your child doesn't misbehave or make poor decisions? Definitely not. But it will help him or her cope with the consequences, learn from mistakes (with your mindful guidance), and find ways to soothe themselves and manage their emotions.

In case you're not familiar with the concept of mindfulness, or are not exactly sure what it means, let's review what it is and how it applies to parenting.

What Is Mindfulness Exactly?

You've probably heard and read a lot about mindfulness recently. There are hundreds of books, magazines, websites, and podcasts devoted to the subject for those seeking the myriad of mental, physical, and emotional benefits mindfulness affords.

Mindfulness practices have their roots in ancient religious traditions, but in today's Western culture, mindfulness has become a more secular practice that can be expressed through many activities. Some of these include:

- Mindfulness meditation
- Guided meditation
- Mindful breathing
- Thought observation
- Body awareness
- Yoga, qigong, and other ascetic disciplines
- Visualization
- Affirmations

In addition to these activities, there are dozens of ways to practice mindfulness in your daily life. In fact, you can be mindful in almost everything you do—from washing the dishes to driving carpool.

As we mention in our book *10-Minute Mindfulness*,[1] "Mindfulness is very simple. It means you become *intentionally aware* of the

---

1 https://www.amazon.com/10-Minute-Mindfulness-Habits-Living-Present -ebook/dp/B071HVMVVR

present moment, while paying close attention to your feelings, thoughts, and sensations of the body."

You are fully available to experience whatever the moment brings without judgment or distraction.

But you've likely noticed that your mind and emotions don't always cooperate with your efforts to be fully attentive to the task or interaction at hand. Your "monkey mind" is easily distracted and pulled from thought to thought. These random thoughts can create negative emotions that further pull you away from whatever you are doing.

It's hard to tame your "monkey mind" so that you control your thoughts rather than your thoughts controlling you. Mindfulness practices (especially meditation) help you harness your thoughts so that you can enjoy the moment rather than getting lost in past regrets or future worries—or current distractions.

Mindfulness also helps you become more proactive and thoughtful about everything you do because you aren't dealing with the mental "clutter" of reactionary thoughts and behaviors. Mindfulness teaches you to pay attention, slow down, and become more creative rather than reactionary.

What Is Mindful Parenting?

As a parent, you may find it especially daunting to be present, intentional, and attentive. You're pulled in dozens of different directions by the many demands on your time and energy. And your children instinctively know how to push every reactive button you possess.

They can sniff out when your emotional bandwidth is low and choose that moment to present their less-than-adorable selves. It's no wonder you see red-faced parents losing it when their children have public meltdowns or getting rankled when their preschoolers sulk at the dinner table.

It's hard not to react (or overreact) to your child's shenanigans, especially when you're stressed and overwhelmed. But even at your best, you'll find it challenging to know what to do and how to respond in irritating, emotionally charged, or embarrassing situations with your kids.

Fortunately, mindful parenting offers a roadmap to help you navigate the challenges and conflicts you'll face with your child without losing it or saying something you later regret.

According to Justin Parent, lead author of a University of Vermont study[2] on how mindful parenting impacts children's well-being, mindful parenting involves three key factors:

1. Noticing your own emotions when you and your child have conflict.
2. Learning to pause before responding to your child in anger.

---

2   https://www.ncbi.nlm.nih.gov/pubmed/25633828

3. Listening carefully to your child's viewpoint, even if you disagree with it.

Practicing these skills not only helps you maintain your close connection with your child but also teaches your child how to respond in a healthy way during difficult situations.

We also believe mindful parenting involves some additional skills that will support your efforts at being the kind of parent you want to be while raising happy, healthy, and successful children. These include:

- Practicing mindfulness-based activities (like meditation) on your own so that you strengthen your ability to be present and attentive in general, which will in turn support your mindful parenting efforts.

- Being proactive with your spouse or partner (or alone, if you aren't co-parenting) to determine your parenting and family values and how you want to apply them with your children.

- Remaining flexible and nimble so you can adapt your parenting skills to your children's developmental stages and to each child's unique emotional needs.

It's important to note a critical distinction between mindful parenting and simply practicing mindfulness as an individual. Both will help you be more present and intentional, and less stressed.

However, practicing mindfulness alone (through meditation, yoga, etc.) isn't enough to handle the emotionally charged situations you'll encounter as a parent. You'll need to learn skills that are specific to mindful parenting.

By taking the time to read this book and learn more about being a mindful parent, you are revealing an important core value for yourself and your family. You want to be more than a caregiver and disciplinarian—you want to be present with your children in good times and bad, and model for them how mindfulness makes life richer, less stressful, and more satisfying.

As a result, you and your children will enjoy unique and long-lasting benefits that will impact your relationship as parent and child and provide a foundation for your child's well-being as he or she grows to adulthood.

The 10 Benefits of Mindfulness

By attending to our deepest selves day to day, we not only receive nourishment but also plant the seeds of a much-needed alternative to prevailing cultural norms. May our inner work be a blessing, and may it help to bring about a more life-giving, just, and peaceful world for ourselves and one another, for our children, for our planet, for our future.

— Abby Seixas, *Finding the Deep River Within: A Woman's Guide to Recovering Balance and Meaning in Everyday Life*

There are so many science-backed benefits to adding mindfulness to your life, both as a parent and an individual.

Let's review a few of them (some of which we include from our book *10-Minute Mindfulness*) so you can see how important mindfulness and mindful parenting is for you, your children, and your family.

1. Mindfulness reduces rumination and overthinking.

Rumination is a maladaptive form of self-reflection that has an addictive quality. When you're constantly "in your head," looping negative thoughts, brooding, and thinking about the past, you put yourself at a much greater risk for mental health problems like depression and anxiety.

Rumination pulls you away from being present and emotionally available to your children. But research studies support the idea that practicing mindfulness helps reduce rumination. In a study[3] by Chambers et al. (2008), participants (with no previous

---

3   https://rd.springer.com/article/10.1007/s10608-007-9119-0

meditation experience) in a mindfulness meditation retreat reported significantly higher mindfulness, less rumination, and fewer symptoms of depression than the control group.

2. Mindfulness alleviates stress.

Stress is inevitable when you have children. The demands on your time, energy, and emotions can take a toll on you and your relationship with your spouse or partner.

A mindfulness practice can decrease the levels of the stress hormone cortisol, according to the results of the Chambers et al. study (as well as numerous other studies). The study shows a direct connection between resting cortisol and scores on a mindfulness scale.

3. Mindfulness helps with emotional reactivity.

Mindfulness helps you deal with your reactions to parenting stress and manage emotional reactivity—and model this behavior for your children. You'll learn to pause before lashing out at your kids and calm yourself down so you can respond more thoughtfully.

According to research[4] presented by the American Mindfulness Research Association, "One advantage of being mindful is that it allows one to respond to situations with equanimity rather than reacting emotionally in a 'knee-jerk fashion.'"

This is reinforced by a study by Ortner et al. (2007)[5] showing that mindfulness meditation allowed participants to disengage from

4   https://goamra.org/emotional-reactivity-lessens-mindfulness-brain-study
-shows/
5   https://link.springer.com/article/10.1007/s11031-007-9076-7

emotionally upsetting pictures and focus better on a cognitive task, as compared with people who saw the pictures but did not practice mindfulness meditation.

4. Mindfulness creates happier relationships.

The research[6] is conclusive that having children negatively impacts relationship satisfaction between couples. But mindfulness can help offset the stressors of raising children so you and your spouse can be better parents and happier partners.

5. Mindfulness reduces anxiety.

Anger, stress, frustration, meltdowns, fear, and anxiety will be regular visitors in your household throughout the years you're a parent.

Mindfulness practices help shrink the amygdala[7]—the fear center of the brain. The practices increase the prefrontal cortex to promote a calmer, steadier brain.

The practice of detachment from and non-judgment of anxious thoughts and feelings helps lessen fearful reactivity to these thoughts.

6. Mindfulness improves sleep.

Insomnia and sleep problems are common stress reactions, and they are also common problems for parents of babies and young children. Mindfulness habits promote calm and reduce rumination that can disrupt sleep.

---

6   https://www.ncbi.nlm.nih.gov/pmc/articles/PMC2702669/
7   https://blogs.scientificamerican.com/guest-blog/what-does-mindfulness-meditation-do-to-your-brain/

A 2015 study[8] of older adults confirms that mindfulness meditation practices support getting a better night's sleep. According to the study, mindfulness meditation can "increase the relaxation response through its function of increasing attentional factors that impart control over the autonomic nervous system."

Mindfulness may not prevent the middle-of-the-night demands from your child, but it can help you fall back asleep more quickly once you return to bed. It can also help you manage worrisome thoughts about older children that can keep you up at night.

7. Mindfulness helps you appreciate your children.

Your time with your children is fleeting, even though the days while you're raising them feel long and are often stressful. The endearing, lovable, clever things your children do today, in this moment, will never return. That is why it is important to recognize how valuable and precious your time with them is.

Mindfulness helps you remain present with your kids and allows you to savor the joy they add to your life. With mindful parenting, you prioritize building deep connections with your children in the relatively short time they are under your care.

8. Mindfulness can be taught to your children.

Mindfulness doesn't have to be a solitary activity reserved for adults. It can be passed down to the next generation, as you help your kids pay attention to the world around them and learn how to better deal with stress and difficult emotions.

---

8   https://jamanetwork.com/journals/jamainternalmedicine/fullarticle/211
0998

According to Lisa Firestone, Ph.D., writing for *Psychology Today*,[9] "Teaching mindfulness practices to our kids helps grow their middle prefrontal cortex, the part of the brain that regulates the body, promotes attuned communication, strengthens the 'pause button,' creates emotional balance, calms fears and incites empathy, intuition and morality—all characteristics we'd like our children to be equipped with throughout their lives."

9. Mindfulness helps you deal with parent-child conflict.

One of the key elements of mindfulness is learning how to pause and listen. This is an important skill to have as a parent, as it teaches you how to pay attention to your kids and what they're trying to communicate to you, even in times of anger or meltdowns.

Although you're the parent and it's your job to guide and discipline your kids, mindfulness allows you to pause and listen to your child with a discerning ear rather than just reacting to bad behavior.

Sometimes your child acts out because he feels frustrated and can't articulate his inner world. Mindfulness helps you go deeper and understand the emotions behind the behavior.

10. Mindful parenting can protect your children.

According to new research,[10] the practices of mindful parenting can protect your kids from anxiety, acting out, and even drug use as they grow and become adolescents.

---

9   https://www.psychologytoday.com/us/blog/compassion-matters/201311/the-rewards-mindful-parenting
10   https://www.ncbi.nlm.nih.gov/pubmed/25633828

In the study, those parents who reported more mindful parenting styles and used more positive and less negative parenting behavior saw more positive behavior in their kids—with fewer mental health issues and better outcomes in general.

Researchers also found that parents who showed more mindful parenting had fewer negative emotions and more shared positive emotion with their children than those lower in mindful parenting.

In general, mindfulness practices and mindful parenting give your family more breathing room and calm. These practices allow you to get below the surface of the situation at hand to make more thoughtful and compassionate decisions.

You gain the freedom to recognize and accept your limitations and be kinder to yourself as a parent. Mindfulness permits the entire family to slow down, enjoy the moment, cherish your time together, and savor the little things that are so intrinsically valuable.

When you extend mindfulness to your parenting style and interactions with your children, you foster an environment in your home that will result in happier, healthier, and more successful children.

According to research[11] published in the *Clinical Child and Family Psychology Review*, mindful parenting is a framework that significantly improves the happiness and relationship satisfaction of both children and parents:

> Our model of mindful parenting suggests that parents who can remain aware and accepting of their child's needs

---

11   https://www.ncbi.nlm.nih.gov/pmc/articles/PMC2730447/

through using mindfulness practices can create a family context that allows for more enduring satisfaction and enjoyment in the parent-child relationship. This view of mindful parenting suggests that parents who either have a natural capacity for, or learn practices of mindfulness will be more likely to develop higher-quality relationships with their children and more often avoid cycles of maladaptive parenting behavior that stem from automatic behaviors and hedonic motivations. This view is a substantial shift from operant behavioral models, and we believe that it is one that can allow for the cultivation of more open and trusting family relationships and parenting styles that will promote the healthy psychosocial development of the child. (Baumrind 1989)

Throughout this book, we detail simple strategies for applying mindfulness to your role as a parent, as well as showing you how mindfulness can enhance your relationship with your spouse or partner (if you have one) and make you a happier, more centered person in general.

If these benefits convince you that mindful parenting is vital to the health, happiness, and success of your children, and to your happiness and success as a parent, then hopefully you're motivated to learn the skills involved.

Remember, perfection is not the goal here. Rather, it's developing more intentionality, awareness, calm, and joy in the wondrous privilege of raising a child.

Barrie's Parenting Story

As the mother of three twenty-somethings, I'm on the precipice of ending my journey of parenting. We say "precipice" because in many ways it feels like falling off a cliff.

For the last twenty-seven years, my identity has been inextricably bound to my role as a parent. Once, my daily life was consumed with my children. Now they are young adults, and my role as a parent has shifted dramatically.

It's rewarding to interact with my kids as adults and to watch them make their way in the world. But it's also scary to watch and have no control—to allow them to "fail forward" when necessary.

It's also scary to recognize that, when it comes to my children, I must create a new identity for myself. As bumpy as the parenting journey is, the post-parenting journey has its own set of challenges.

Having been through all of the stages of child-rearing with three very different children, I have a unique perspective to bring to this book. I can look back at my successes and failures as a parent and recognize where more mindful parenting would have saved both me and my children from some head-spinning moments.

Fortunately, I can also look back and remember times when I was fully present as a parent. One memory in particular stands out as I write this section. My son (and middle child) was an infant, and he awakened in the middle of the night crying and hungry. After feeding him, I tried rocking him to sleep, but nothing would do except for standing up and walking with him. Every time I tried to sit (as I was exhausted), he would scream. Stand up, calm. Sit down, scream.

I remember staring out the window, looking at the full moon while his little head was on my shoulder, and thinking, "Remember this. You'll never have a moment like this again with him. Don't focus on your exhaustion. Be here with John and savor this." Now, twenty-five years later, I remember that moment like it was yesterday.

At the time, I didn't know about mindfulness and had never heard of "mindful parenting." In fact, the parenting style of the day encouraged us to engage our children in a multitude of scheduled activities and hover around them like "helicopter parents," ensuring they didn't suffer the horrors of failure or low self-esteem.

I also thought multitasking and getting chores done while trying to interact with my children was a valuable, Super Mom skill. Looking back, I wish I'd had the insight to make things simpler and less structured for my kids. I also wish that I'd had the awareness to slow down, live with a messier house, and enjoy more special time with each child.

Every generation of parents tries to do better than the generation before. Every generation of parents seeks guidance and wisdom from the parenting gurus and trends of the day. But over the years, I have come to believe that the best judge of good parenting styles are the parents themselves.

You know yourself and your children. You know what you want your home life to look and feel like. Your inner wisdom and life values are your best guides, and when you rely on them and your knowledge of your child, you're on the right track.

That's the essence of mindful parenting—having both the awareness and confidence to do what you think is best for you, your child, and your family, even if you make a few mistakes along the way.

Today's generation of parents have more distractions than ever. You're raising kids in a digital age that creates a unique set of challenges I didn't have to face when my children were young.

Now, more than ever, you will be faced with balancing the ever-present intrusion of media and technology with raising happy, centered, and confident children. Steve and I hope this book and our backgrounds as parents and mindfulness authors will help you achieve that.

Steve's Parenting Story

I'm a work-from-home father of two boys—one a very, *very* active toddler and one newborn. So my days involve all the "joys" of helping raise young children. From toddler meltdowns, to potty training, to a screaming baby, my wife and I are constantly moving from one crisis to another.

This current experience has taught me the importance of enjoying these crazy, stressful times. Sure, it's not always pleasant listening to my toddler son having a meltdown after he spills a drink on his favorite giraffe blanket. But I also recognize that "this too shall pass." In other words, even though dealing with small children can be stressful, there will be a time in the future when I'll look back at this time with fondness.

Furthermore, I have learned many valuable lessons from other parents about staying in the present moment. After reading a great article called "The Tail End,"[12] I vowed to enjoy life *right now*, instead of constantly looking to the future. This means working less, planning fun day trips for my family, and generally enjoying the short amount of time I have with my young children.

What I've come to realize is that mindfulness is important for both parents *and* children. Not only does it help my wife and I navigate those chaotic moments, it also provides an example to our sons of how to positively respond to stress and anxiety. Our hope is that the lessons and activities (that we discuss throughout the book) will be something our sons will remember with fondness when they get older.

---

12   https://waitbutwhy.com/2015/12/the-tail-end.html

As you can see, both Barrie and I have a wide range of experiences when it comes to living in the present moment while raising children in a stressful environment. So let's move on and talk about what you will learn in the following book that we've titled *Mindful Parenting Habits: 26 Practices for Raising Your Child with More Presence and Less Stress (From Infancy to Kindergarten)*.

Mindful Parenting for the Early Years

This book will cover mindfulness for parents with young children. Specifically, we will talk about the unique challenges and mindful parenting skills you'll need for each of the following stages:

- Infants and babies
- Toddlers
- Preschool-aged children

Our hope is that you'll view mindfulness and mindful parenting as an ongoing core value in your family that guides you through all of these stages (and beyond), and that you'll teach your children age-appropriate mindfulness skills as they grow.

For the sake of convenience, we cover specific parenting requirements for each of these developmental stages. But you'll see how many of the strategies presented apply *to all stages*—both to the way you parent and what you teach your child about mindfulness.

The practices of being attentive, intentional, and compassionate will serve you whether you are waking in the middle of the night with a crying infant or dealing with back-talk from a sulky 'tween.

You may be the parent of an only child, or have two or more children of different ages and stages. Wherever you are on the parenting journey and whatever age your child (or children) happens to be, we encourage you to read through *all of the mindful parenting skills* presented here for each age group.

You'll find nuggets of inspiration and actionable ideas in each section that you can use for yourself, pass on to your children, and share with friends, siblings, and other family members who have children of their own.

Even if you're currently in the later stages of parenting, it's helpful to review the strategies for some of the earlier age groups. You'll recognize where you've successfully applied mindful parenting in the past and understand where you can improve going forward. It's never too late to be a mindful parent.

Reflecting on your parenting journey and acknowledging your successes and failures can promote more closeness, connection, and compassion with your children. Being open to learning and growing as a parent is a mindfulness practice in and of itself.

Further, the benefit of hindsight positions you as a seasoned mentor to parents with younger children who can learn from the wisdom and experience you bring to the table and find inspiration from the values of mindful parenting you model.

Bottom line: Whether you are rocking a baby or sending your child off to kindergarten, we hope you'll read the entirety of this book to gain the most from it for yourself, your kids, your family, and your sphere of influence.

So let's start the conversation about the many challenges that you are probably facing right now.

The Top 10 Challenges of Being a Parent

Before Steve and Barrie had their first children, they both recall thinking, *How hard can it be to have an infant in the house?*

They just need to be fed, changed, and rocked. They can't talk back or get into mischief. They sleep most of the time, and when they're awake, they wave their little arms and legs around and make happy noises. What's the big deal?

It's hard to understate the naiveté of their assumptions. A baby turns your world upside down and triggers a years-long state of exhaustion you can't anticipate. And once you think you've finally mastered the infant stage, you're in for other big surprises when your baby starts walking, hits the "terrible twos," or begins potty training.

Every stage is challenging and surprising in its own way. Although you will enjoy periods of relative calm and ease with parenting, you can't become too complacent. Another set of challenges awaits you at the next turn.

It's these challenges that test our resolve as parents who value a mindful approach to child-rearing. Committing to mindful parenting is one thing—acting on it is quite another, especially when you're in the trenches and trying to craft a response to your screaming banshee that doesn't involve chugging whiskey straight from the bottle and setting yourself on fire.

Over the last few decades, parenting styles and the relation-ship between parents and children have changed profoundly. Although parents now spend more time with their children and have closer bonds with them in adulthood, they also deal with more anxieties, guilt, and conflicting advice than their predecessors.

The clear and authoritative guidelines set by parenting experts in earlier decades (like Dr. Benjamin Spock) have given way to inconsistent messages about how much to involve yourself in your child's activities and academic endeavors. You're unsure whether or not to provide less structure with more free time for your child to explore the world.

In addition, today's culture is more complicated, competitive, and fraught with distractions and potential perils (cyberbullying, sexting, "stranger danger," etc.) than any previous generation. As a result, you're faced with challenges that your parents and grandparents couldn't have imagined.

If this sounds like a depressing characterization of life for today's parents, that's not our intention. We don't mean to paint an alarming picture of your experience raising your kids. But you do have to contend with some issues unique to parenting trends over the past few decades, cultural changes related to marriage and work, and easy access of technology in virtually every corner of our lives.

Just so you're completely clear about what you're up against, let's review the top ten challenges parents face in this complex Information Age.

Challenge 1: Lack of Time

Most moms and dads today work full-time jobs with dual incomes. As a result, parenting has become a juggling act in which you're struggling to balance conflicting demands on your time and energy.

A single parent has even less time to devote to child-rearing. The percentage of children in the U.S. living with single parents has more than doubled since 1968, jumping from 13% to 32% in 2017, according to the Pew Research Center.[13]

Parents don't have enough time for self-care because when they are home, they feel they should spend every minute engaged with their children. This lack of time leaves parents feeling guilty, exhausted, stressed out, and worried they aren't doing *anything* well. Maybe you can relate.

Challenge 2: Emotional Demands

Whether they are infants, teenagers, or any age in between, your children will frequently exert their emotional needs and make emotional demands on you that feel overwhelming.

Some of these emotional reactions relate to cultural changes children face today with ever-present digital devices, little free time or time spent outdoors, and increasing pressure to perform at school and with extracurricular activities.

Behaviors like temper tantrums, whining, arguing, back-talking, and insults will test you to your limits. As hard as you try to stay calm and composed when your child has an emotional outburst, you will often feel at a loss for how to best respond.

Sometimes your child's emotional demands will trigger strong emotions in you that you can't control. You may lose your temper, say things you regret, or inflict knee-jerk punishments that aren't well-considered. All of this adds to the emotional turmoil in your home.

---

13   https://www.pewresearch.org/fact-tank/2018/04/27/about-one-third-of -u-s-children-are-living-with-an-unmarried-parent/

Challenge 3: Aggression

When your child gets emotionally flooded, his or her feelings may come out in aggressive behaviors, especially if he or she regularly witnesses aggression in others.

Hitting you or other children, being destructive, kicking, exhibiting intense anger, and picking fights are behaviors that can trigger your own fight-or-flight responses if you don't know how to handle your child's intensity.

Challenge 4: Judgment from Others

Family members, friends, and parenting experts all have opinions about the "right" way to raise your kids. You may have people in your life who believe they're helping you by telling you what you're doing wrong and how you need to change.

Comments like, "Why aren't you breastfeeding?" or "In my day, we'd let the baby cry it out," can make you feel defensive and doubt your own judgment.

In addition, social media can be another guilt- or shame-inducing forum when you see other parents (and their "superstar" children) who feel the need to share their parenting doctrines and why they are more successful than all of the other loser parents out there.

Feelings of judgment and peer pressure can cause you to feel insecure about your parenting, and may even compel you to send mixed messages to your children—something they will pick up on and use to their advantage.

Challenge 5: Seeking Perfection

Judgment from others on your parenting is bad enough, but self-judgment can erode your confidence and undermine the joy of being a mom or dad.

You may have a vision of what it means to be a "perfect" parent, and when you fall short of that vision, you feel like a failure—like you've failed your child.

Previous generations of parents didn't feel as responsible for their children's success, self-esteem, and happiness. But you want to protect your kids from pain, failure, disappointment, and heartache.

As a result, today's children don't often encounter the natural consequences, challenges, and setbacks that are an important part of learning and becoming a self-sufficient adult.

Challenge 6: Technology and Screen Time

Constant connectivity through computers, television, electronic games, and cell phones is creating a generation of children who can't disconnect from the digital world.

As a parent, you're torn between the convenience of these modern-day, child entertainment (and babysitting) devices and the knowledge that too much time on them can cause a host of issues, including attention deficit disorder, learning problems, anxiety and depression, and speech or language delays, according to research.[14]

There's so much pressure from peers, television, and social

---

14 https://www.longdom.org/open-access/the-impact-of-using-gadgets-on
-children-2167-1044-1000296.pdf

media, that trying to manage your child's digital time feels like an uphill battle.

Challenge 7: Over-Scheduling

Today's parents feel less comfortable than previous generations of parents allowing their children the untethered freedom to play outside and roam short distances away from home on their bikes. There are too many real and imagined dangers to allow that kind of autonomy.

Parents are also more performance-focused and worry that their child won't survive in our competitive economy if Mom and Dad don't intervene early and often.

As a result, parents invest more and more time (and money) into arranged playdates, enrichment classes, and extracurricular activities to ensure their children have every advantage.

But this overscheduling creates more stress and pressure for both parents and children and doesn't allow kids to just be kids. Many high-achieving young adults are suffering from anxiety, depression, and other mental illnesses in an effort to rise to parental and self-expectations.

Challenge 8: Not Listening

One of the most common complaints you hear from parents is that their children don't listen. Getting your kids to pay attention and follow instructions feels like herding fleas.

Often, you repeat the same request a dozen times before it sinks in (or it's acknowledged) and your child takes action. You resort to nagging or yelling to get his or her attention, but then you feel guilty and bad about yourself for losing your temper.

The old rule, "I'm just going to say this once..." no longer applies. Your child is too distracted or doesn't fear the consequences, and therefore tunes you out. You feel conflicted and out of control.

Challenge 9: Letting Go

As your child gets older, it's natural that he or she will gain more and more independence and accept more personal responsibility. You want to trust your kids, but you also know all the ways they can screw up and jeopardize their own paths to success.

You want to protect your children from harm, poor decisions, and mistakes, but if you want them to learn valuable life lessons, you must let go and allow them to "fail forward" if necessary.

Many parents find this process the most challenging of all, as they have invested so much time and energy into their children that it's hard to bear the thought of their children squandering their efforts with one bad decision.

Challenge 10: Failure to Launch

There is an epidemic of young adult children who "fail to launch," still living at home or depending on parents emotionally and financially long after they should be self-sufficient and managing adult responsibilities.

You may not be worried about this challenge now, when your child hasn't even reached their teen years, but it's wise to recognize this problem is real. It's never too early to teach your kids the practical skills they need to become independent adults—beginning with natural consequences, personal responsibility, and saving money.

As a result of creating child-centered environments at home or protecting their kids from consequences, parents can find themselves in the untenable position of pushing their child out of the nest rather than watching them fly away with ease.

Because we remove obstacles from our children's lives and do backflips to ensure their happiness during childhood, young adults often don't have the coping skills to face real-world challenges. As they flounder, you are left wondering, "What did I do wrong? I gave them everything!"

You may have already faced some of these challenges in your family and with your child. Others may be waiting for you down the road, as your child enters new developmental stages. And perhaps you will escape the worst of these difficulties, or they will be relatively minor bumps in the road.

Being prepared for the possibility of these common parenting challenges is the best way to mitigate the potential disruptions and discord, as you can devise your planned responses, rules, and consequences before the situations ever arise.

This forethought and deliberation is an essential part of mindful parenting, allowing you to be more creative and thoughtful rather than reactive and emotional.

The foundation for this planning rests in the guiding principles or values you hold dear as parents—and how you intend to apply these principles with your child. Defining your values as parents will give you a roadmap for who you want to be with your children and keep you on the high road during the inevitable storms that will arise on the journey.

So let's talk about how to define *your* values next.

What Are Your Mindful Parenting Values?

Before we discuss each developmental stage and the related mindfulness skills, we believe it's essential that you craft your parenting values and develop a general "family philosophy" to serve as a blueprint for your choices, decisions, ground rules, and consequences. Please take some time to read this section and identify these values before you move on to the next sections of the book.

Rather than just "winging it" as you go, or depending entirely on parenting gurus or advice from friends and family, remember that *you* are the experts on *your* child. And only you know the kind of environment and principles that are important to you.

If you have a spouse or co-parent, do this exercise together, as it's essential the two of you are on the same page when it comes to child-rearing and the type of home life you want to foster for yourselves and your children.

Being intentional about these values can save you time, emotional energy, and even heartache down the road. It also inspires you to set standards for yourselves as parents (and as a couple) and helps you stay accountable to those standards on a daily basis.

Parenting your children and building a secure and happy home life for them is the most important job you'll ever undertake. If you enter it—or continue it—without any forethought or preparation, you're allowing in-the-moment circumstances and emotions to determine how you want to respond and make decisions.

Creating this blueprint is a mindfulness activity that ensures you have plans and tools available when you need them in high-stress moments. It also helps you shape your decisions about how you create boundaries for your children, how you choose to nurture and guide them, and how you spend your time as a family.

One of the best ways to discern your parenting values and guiding principles is through self-questioning.

Your answers to the questions we provide here will help you determine the actions you intend to take, both preemptively and in real time, to support your mindful parenting commitment.

After you answer these questions and define actions, your next step will be to review the values and actions on a weekly or bi-monthly basis to ensure you're staying on track and making any necessary course corrections.

Your family and parenting values may shift over time as your children grow and your lives change, so revisit them yearly to ensure they are still relevant and aligned with your principles for your family.

We suggest you and your spouse review the following questions and write your answers in a journal. Share your answers with each other and devise one value statement that reflects both answers or a compromise you decide on together. Then brainstorm specific actions you will take to support your value statements.

For example, for question one, "What is the general atmosphere you want in your home?" your value statement might be:

We want our home to be a place of calm and peace in which we prioritize quality time together, encourage healthy self-expression, and spend time talking, sharing, enjoying fun activities, and giving ourselves the time and space to recharge and find emotional balance.

Action steps you determine based on this value statement might be something like:

- We will take a family walk, play a game, or do some activity together every day.

- Mom and Dad will spend thirty minutes before dinner each evening talking alone while the children play or read quietly.

- We will watch only one hour of television as a family each evening.

- The children are allowed two hours per week of computer time.

- Our dinner hour is a sacred time where we share the events of the day. We don't bring negativity or conflict to the table, and phones (and other distractions) are put away.

- We will not yell or raise our voices in our home, even in anger.

- We will practice a five-minute meditation with the children before bed.

- We will be fully present for each other (without distractions) when talking together and listen attentively when one of us needs to speak.

As you read through the remainder of this book, you may want to go back and revise your value statements or add/change some of the related actions. Some questions may stump you right now or may not apply to your child's current stage. You can skip them and return to them later when you have more clarity or when they are more relevant to your child's age.

Remember, the value statements and actions you define are your best *intentions and goals*, but we know that parenting is challenging and can trip up even the most committed and mindful among us.

There will be plenty of times when you fall short of your intentions as a mindful parent, but please don't beat yourself up over it. You are devising these values and actions to help you do your best—not to be a perfect parent.

Grab your journal or notebook and a pen, and let's get started.

Here are the self-questions to help you clarify your parenting and family values:

- What is the general atmosphere you want in your home?
- What balance do you want to create between children, work, personal time, and other commitments and activities?
- How do you want your children to see you and your partner interacting together?
- What is your philosophy on discipline and rewards for your child?
- What is your philosophy on corporal punishment?
- Under what circumstances would you need to apologize to your child?

- Ideally, how do you want to react or behave when your child is misbehaving, breaking rules, or acting out?

- In general, how do you want to speak to your child?

- In general, how do you want your child to feel when he or she is in your home?

- What is your personal commitment to understanding and learning about the typical needs and behaviors that accompany your child's stage of development?

- How can you best support and nurture your child's mental and emotional health?

- How will you know when your family life is out of balance?

- What is your philosophy on accumulating material things (toys, clothes, etc.) for your child?

- What is your philosophy on the use of digital devices and television for your child?

- What are the most important values you want to teach (and model for) your child?

- What kind of education do you want for your child?

- What is your philosophy about extracurricular activities (type and how many) for your child?

- What is your philosophy about your younger child or baby sleeping in your room or bed?

- What is your philosophy about your home being more child-centered versus parent-centered?

- What is your philosophy about childcare (if it's necessary)?

- What is your philosophy about food and food choices for your child?

- What is the division of labor plan for maintaining your home for both children and parents?

- What are your homework and academic expectations for your child?

- How involved do you need to be in your child's academic work and achievements?

- In what ways and how often should you express your love to your child?

- What is your philosophy about manners for your child?

- What parenting mistakes do you most want to avoid?

- What character traits do you desire most for your child?

- Under what circumstances would you intervene to protect your child from consequences resulting from a bad choice or decision?

- What spiritual or religious beliefs do you want to teach your child?

- What are the top life lessons you want to teach your child?

- What do you want to teach your child about sex?

- What do you want to teach your child about alcohol and recreational drug use?

- What are your top five priorities as parents?

- What do you want the most for your child?

Now that you have a general picture of your parenting and family values, let's dive into the mindful parenting skills for each of three developmental stages for young children. But before we move on, we want to remind you to refer back to your values regularly, discuss them with your spouse or partner, and make changes based on what you're learning about yourselves and your child.

Let's start the conversation by talking about how to be mindful with your brand-new bundle of joy.

INFANTS AND BABIES
(AGES: 0–12 MONTHS)

If you're a new parent with a baby, you may wonder if mindful parenting applies to you. How can you be intentional with an infant whose needs are often unpredictable and sometimes indiscernible?

Where you were once an accomplished multitasker, you've probably quickly discovered that you can do little else beyond being available when your baby needs you—which is 24/7. Your time is no longer your own, and you have no choice but to give up control of your schedule, your environment, and your sleep.

Mothers in particular face overwhelming physical, mental, and emotional demands when an infant enters the home. In addition to the emotional rollercoaster of pregnancy and childbirth, Mom must learn how to feed and care for the baby while coping with her postpartum health and emotional well-being.

Dads have their own sets of challenges, sometimes feeling left out, exhausted, or incompetent related to caring for a new baby. Life as you once knew it feels upended and chaotic. The closest thing to nirvana these days is getting a few blessed hours of sleep.

Despite the struggles and exhaustion, the infancy stage is the best time to learn to be a mindful parent, especially if this is your first child. The loss of control and the sudden toppling of your former lives requires that you either let go or risk feeling constantly resentful and overwhelmed.

If you choose to let go and be present during this intense stage, there's no doubt it's a shocking immersion into mindfulness—but one that sets the stage for your future as relaxed, intentional, and joyful parents.

As your newborn develops into a sturdy and alert baby, some of the physical demands on you may diminish. Your baby may be sleeping through the night and have gotten past the colicky stage. You've likely figured out some routines or developed a workable schedule that affords more predictability to your lives.

Your growing baby is beginning to notice the world around him. If all goes well, he's hitting developmental milestones that are thrilling to witness—holding up his head, rolling over, sitting up, and laughing. You begin to feel that a real, unique person is developing before your eyes.

You may still be exhausted, have anxiety if your baby fails to hit those milestones on time, or feel conflicted about letting your baby "cry it out." But in those months before your little one takes his first steps, you will take great delight in being a parent if you practice mindfulness.

What to Expect during This Stage

During the first three months, your baby is awake about one hour in every ten—although it probably seems she may have different sleep hours than you do. She depends on you for everything and can barely support her own head.

By three months, your baby has more control over her body and has started to notice things, including her own hands and feet. She begins to laugh and coo, and she's delighted when you talk or read to her. Your baby can remain alert for fifteen or more minutes at a time.

Between three and five months, your baby is developing rapidly and may be able to roll over and sit with support. She can hold toys and try to grab them when they are put out of reach. She will start to babble and can stay alert for two or more hours at a time.

Your baby is on the go by nine or ten months, crawling and pulling up on furniture. She loves to explore, grasp objects, and be with other babies and children. And she can understand simple commands from you.

At twelve months, your baby is curious about everything and wants to explore and learn by getting messy. She may be saying, "Mama" and "Dada," and is making lots of sounds—maybe even saying a few other words. If she's not yet walking, she is moving around furniture and touching everything. She can play near other babies but not yet play with them.

What Your Baby Needs during This Stage

During the early months, your baby needs a warm crib, a peaceful (and smoke-free) environment, plenty of cuddling and affection, and to hear your loving voice through talking, singing, and reading.

In time, take your baby out for fresh air in the stroller and be sure to offer him plenty of things to teethe on and to create visual stimulation. Safety-proof your home as your baby starts to crawl and touch everything.

Once he is eating solids, offer nutritious food and give him educational toys to stimulate learning. Older babies need lots of encouragement, cuddling, and a bit more freedom to explore. Be sure to continue reading and singing to your baby every day.

These early months in your child's development offer times of unbridled joy and love, as well as feelings of overwhelm and frustration. During the joyful times, you will rely on mindfulness to savor these fleeting and magical moments. When things are rough, mindful parenting gives you the coping mechanisms to get through the challenges smoothly—or at least with your dignity intact.

Now that you know the basics of your baby's development and needs, let's go over some specific mindful parenting skills for this stage.

1. Practice Presence and Awareness

Present moment awareness is the cornerstone of mindfulness, and you will hear us repeat the value of this practice many times throughout this book.

Reality exists only in the present, not in past regrets or worries about the future. To get the most out of any experience, you need to be fully present with it—and that holds particularly true with being a parent.

Your infant is growing so quickly that, from one week to the next, he or she will have gained weight, started smiling, or rolled over before you know it. You may hear grandparents who visit on occasion exclaim, "Oh my, she has gotten so big," or "He was barely holding his head up when I was here last."

You, on the other hand, may not be so aware of these changes. You're with your baby every day, and you may miss the gradual developments because of your exhaustion or the general demands of caring for your infant and dealing with other life responsibilities.

If your baby is a second or third child, the surprise element of each growth milestone may have lost its fascination. You've seen it all before, and maybe you feel a little inured to these expected developmental changes.

There may be times when you are so tired and overwhelmed that you do everything on autopilot, just waiting for the moment when you can crawl into bed or eat a meal sitting down.

But we implore you to make this your mantra during these demanding months: *Be here now.*

Childhood itself is fleeting, and infancy and babyhood are over before you can blink. It may feel long and exhausting right now, but ask most parents of adult children, and you'll hear something like, "I wish I'd paid more attention when they were babies."

During the precious moments when your baby is sleeping, or cooing, or smiling at you so adoringly, it's easy to be present. It's not as easy in the middle of the night when your baby is screaming or while you're changing a diaper so smelly you almost pass out.

How can you be more present during the daunting times as well as the easy ones? It's hard to remember to be present throughout your day, so we suggest that you post reminders around your house.

- Put sticky notes that read, "Be here now" in different rooms where you frequently spend time with your baby (in the nursery, on the rocker, etc.). Even put them on the diaper bag and in the car for times you go out.

- Post them in areas where you spend time alone for self-care or household chores (washing dishes, folding clothes, or sitting outside during baby's nap).

- Allow these reminders to refocus your attention on exactly what you are doing, how you are feeling, and what you notice. As you are feeding your baby, pay attention to the close bond this time together creates and how amazing it is that you are providing the sustenance your baby needs.

- When your baby is fussy or crying, notice how she is trying to communicate a need to you. Acknowledge your own feelings in this moment (helplessness, frustration, worry) without judgment or shame.

- When you're away from your baby, practice this same attentiveness in your other daily activities, rather than going through the motions in an exhausted, numbed-out state.

- Don't ruminate about how tired you are or how overwhelmed you feel. It may seem hard to focus when you're tired, but focus is exactly what you need to distract you from your exhaustion. Envision each chore or daily activity as a microcosm of the gratitude and joy you want in your life.

2. Practice Gratitude

Speaking of gratitude, this time with your baby is one of the most precious gifts you will ever receive—in spite of the physical and emotional demands you're encountering.

As part of practicing presence, notice what you feel grateful for during both the satisfying and difficult moments of your life with a new child. Intentionally direct your thoughts to feelings of gratitude when you feel yourself slipping into frustration, resentment, or overwhelm.

Feelings of gratitude come naturally when your baby sleeps through the night, smiles perfectly when Grandma visits, or doesn't wail in the grocery store. But look for reasons to feel gratitude during the less-than-perfect moments.

- Be grateful your child is crying because she is communicating with you the best way she can.

- Be grateful during the middle-of-the-night feeding because you have a peaceful and sacred moment alone with your baby.

- Be grateful when you have to put down your phone or turn off the TV to tend to your baby. Your devices will always be there, but your time with your child is fleeting.

You may not have time for a full gratitude journaling practice, but you can jot down some daily gratitude bullet points in your baby book or a baby journal. You can include gratitude feelings related to your child, as well as other gratitude moments you experience during these special early days with your child.

For example...

- The sun first peeking through the window as you feed your baby at dawn.
- Your spouse offering to clean the kitchen so you can get some rest.
- Your first sip of coffee in the morning after a long night.
- How liberating it feels to take a walk with your baby on a warm, sunny day.
- The bliss of a warm shower or bath and a hot cup of tea.
- The new diaper pail that is odor-free.
- The delicious dinner your neighbors made for you.

Focusing on feelings of gratitude, rather than on the challenges you may be experiencing, has been proven to strengthen your relationships (with your spouse and others), improve your physical health, help you sleep better, reduce stress, and boost resilience, according to research.[15]

Your positive and grateful frame of mind will also impact your baby, who can sense and react to your emotional cues.

According to Jennifer E. Lansford, PhD, a professor with the Social Science Research Institute and the Center for Child and Family Policy at Duke University,[16] "From birth, infants pick up on emotional cues from others. Even very young infants look to caregivers to determine how to react to a given situation."

---

15   https://www.psychologytoday.com/us/blog/what-mentally-strong-people-dont-do/201504/7-scientifically-proven-benefits-gratitude

16   https://www.firstthingsfirst.org/first-things/babies-sense-parents-emotions-help-understand-world/

3. Incorporate the Three Mindful Breaths Method

You can feel so overwhelmed and anxious in the early days with a baby that it's impossible to practice being present. You are too agitated to focus on anything beyond your stress and exhaustion. When you feel this way, your day can quickly go from bad to worse because you are so emotionally flooded.

Fortunately, you can ground yourself again and return to presence by practicing the *Three Mindful Breaths method*. Just by focusing on your breathing for less than a minute, you move your attention away from your emotions, grounding them in your physical body through the sensations of inhaling and exhaling.

This type of focused breathing helps you relax your mind and body so you can observe and respond mindfully to your baby and to your own needs rather than being emotionally reactive.

This technique also trains your mind and body to let go. Negative and disruptive thoughts and feelings come and go. As you quiet your mind through attentive breathing, these thoughts and feelings lose their power to disturb your emotional equilibrium and disrupt your focus.

Here's how to practice Three Mindful Breaths:

- Find a quiet place to sit or stand and close your eyes for a few seconds. Even if your baby is crying, put him down in a safe place for a few seconds to practice this short exercise (unless it's an urgent situation) so that you can calmly return to him.

- Begin by inhaling a slow, deep breath through your nostrils and into your chest and abdomen. Focus your attention on the air as it travels all the way to your abdomen.

- Next, pay attention as the inhalation ends with a short pause, and then gently exhale, moving the air back from your abdomen, chest, and nostrils. Focus on the breath as it travels all the way back out of your body.

- Repeat this process three times, keeping your mind intently focused on each breath. Don't allow too long of a pause between breaths so your mind doesn't pull your attention away from breathing.

- Instead, between breaths, briefly notice the way your body relaxes and your mind becomes clearer with each full, deep breath.

- At the end of the three breaths, evaluate how you're feeling. If you still feel agitated, take three more breaths following the same instructions.

You may need to practice Three Mindful Breaths several times throughout the day when you're feeling especially overwhelmed. In fact, any time you notice yourself tensing up or becoming agitated, you should return to this exercise.

Even in the midst of chaos, mindful breathing can come to the rescue, offering a brief respite and a soothing antidote for your disconnection with presence.

4. Learn to Let Go

Prior to having children, you might have taken for granted how easy it was to control your environment, your personal needs, your freedom, your sleep, and your schedule. *All* of that changes when you have a baby.

What once took you thirty minutes to accomplish (getting dressed in the morning, unloading and loading the dishwasher, or putting on your makeup), now takes hours—if it gets done at all.

If you're a tidy person, your once spotless home has slipped into chaos. Your hair is unkempt, and there's always a baby puke stain on your clothes. Just making it to the grocery store seems to take a Herculean effort.

You're operating on half the sleep you need to function optimally, and if you are a mom, you may be dealing with leaky breasts, postpartum pain, and extra baby weight.

The buttoned-up adult part of you wants to reclaim the order and control you once had over your life. You really want to enjoy your baby, but you also want to look presentable, eat a decent meal, and have a clean home.

You may try to push through and do all these things while soothing your baby or instead of taking that much-needed nap. **This is where mindful parenting should kick in—not only for your baby's sake but also for your own sanity**.

Remember, infancy and babyhood don't last long. You will have plenty of time down the road to focus on your home, your chores, and your appearance.

Right now, your priorities are tending to your baby's needs, enjoying your time with her, getting some sleep, eating healthy, and having some time with your spouse or partner. Everything else can fall by the wayside or at least way down your priority list.

- If you feel agitated by your messy house, practice the Three Mindful Breaths and step over the mess.

- If you look in the mirror and think you look like a refugee, remind yourself that you're prioritizing the most important things right now.

- If you feel overwhelmed by the untended chores or tasks waiting for you, acknowledge that you need to let them go for now or hire someone to help you.

Don't miss out on these miraculous, precious early days with your baby because the rest of your life isn't in perfect order. No one is judging you, so please don't judge yourself for taking a temporary hiatus from your previous standards.

If you need a reminder, post a sign on your refrigerator or bathroom mirror that reads, "Let it go." Then practice that. You don't need to be Super Mom or Dad. You need to be present, rested, and healthy—and for most new parents, that is a full plate.

5. Prioritize Self-Care

This may seem like a contradiction to the previous strategy, but in addition to letting things go, you need to hold tightly to your self-care. Believe it or not, it's an essential part of mindful parenting.

You may wonder how to include self-care in your schedule when you're trying to let go of other important life responsibilities. It feels a bit selfish and indulgent to look after yourself when there is so much to be done. But it's all a matter of carefully prioritizing what is most important and supportive of your parenting values and mental health.

In fact, you may need to recalibrate your priorities on a daily (and sometimes hourly) basis as your baby's requirements and your own physical and emotional needs fluctuate.

Too often, parents put self-care at the bottom of the priority list when it should be at the top. You've heard your flight attendant say it many times, "Put on your own oxygen mask first before assisting others." To have the energy and stamina to be a mindful parent, you need to put self-care first so you can be available for your baby.

That doesn't mean you ignore your baby's cries while you soak in the tub or choose to watch the game rather than cuddling with your infant. But it *does* mean that when you have downtime when your baby is sleeping or someone else is watching her, you use it to nurture yourself.

Here are a number of practices you should focus on to prioritize self-care:

- **Get as much sleep as possible.** Sleep is foundational to effective self-care. Without adequate sleep, nothing else you do will be enough to make up for it. Go to bed earlier, knowing you will likely be awakened during the night or early in the morning. When baby is napping, take a nap yourself rather than doing chores.

- **Exercise a few times per week.** Even if it's just for fifteen minutes, try to go for a short walk, jump on a rebounder at home, or do some jumping jacks. If you can get away for some sustained aerobic exercise, do it. It will energize you and help you maintain your stamina and sanity.

- **Spend time outdoors in quiet reflection.** Time in nature is calming and proven to reduce stress. Step outside to breathe, meditate, or just look at the stars. Even a short walk around your house is a welcome change of atmosphere, allowing you to decompress for a few minutes.

- **Talk to the important people in your life.** It's easy to feel disconnected and isolated when you are spending so much time at home or balancing work and baby care. Make a point to call family and friends and ask them to come by for a visit.

- **Set boundaries with family and friends.** On the other hand, friends and family can sometimes overwhelm you with visits and calls when you have a baby. Too much company can be draining. Learn to say, "Not today. I'm not feeling up to visitors."

- **Delegate.** Let others help you by making meals, tidying up, and watching baby while you nap. You can't do it all, so don't try. Ask for help without embarrassment, and allow family and friends to pitch in.

- **Eat healthy, nourishing meals.** This is particularly important if you're a breastfeeding mom, but both parents need to keep their energy up by eating plenty of vegetables, fruits, whole grains, and lean protein. Simple, easy meals can still be healthy.

- **Connect with your spouse or partner.** Take some time every day to reconnect with your spouse by talking, cuddling, and sharing your feelings. Your relationship will be impacted by a child entering your life, so you must be mindful about nurturing your connection and emotional intimacy.

- **Make feeding times peaceful.** As often as possible, ensure that the time you spend breastfeeding or bottle feeding your baby is a quiet and calming experience. Turn off the TV, put down your phone, and enjoy this special time with your child.

- **Practice positive self-talk.** Whether you're a first-time parent or raising baby number three, you'll find yourself thinking negatively about your parenting skills from time to time. Be intentional about your self-talk by focusing on what you're doing well. Become your own biggest cheerleader and supportive voice.

- **Find some "me" time.** Both Mom and Dad need some time alone to recharge and do something that feels relaxing or energizing. This may be taking a soothing bath, reading a book, meeting a friend for coffee, or joining a quick pick-up game with the guys. Give each other the gift of time alone — or if you're a single parent, ask a friend or family member to watch your baby for an hour or two.

- **Hydrate relentlessly.** A breastfeeding mom needs to drink an extra quart of water (32 ounces) per day beyond the normal eight, eight-ounce glasses a day recommendation. But both parents often forget to hydrate because they are so busy with a baby in the house. Mild dehydration can make you more fatigued, give you headaches, and even make you feel moody, so keep a full water bottle with you to remind you to drink up.

- **Listen to soothing music.** Listening to slow, quiet, classical music can have a relaxing effect on your mind and body. Classical music has been shown to slow the pulse and heart rate, lower blood pressure, and decrease levels of stress hormones. This music can also calm your baby and soothe him to sleep.

- **Savor mindful moments.** Part of your self-care is taking the time to savor the small, positive moments throughout your day. When drinking your morning tea or coffee, savor it rather than gulping it without thought. When your baby is sleeping, take a moment to savor the quiet peace in your house.

- **Use aromatherapy.** Just inhaling the scent of lavender is enough to make you feel calmer and less worried. And citrus smells like lemongrass and grapefruit can make you feel more energetic. Using essential oils is a great way to give yourself a mini spa moment.

- **Unplug from your digital devices.** Take an hour (better yet, three hours) a day to unplug from the internet and all its attractions. Use this time to practice one of the other self-care activities mentioned here or to spend time with your baby.

- **Talk out your feelings.** Whether it's with your spouse, a friend, or a therapist, talk about all of the emotions you're feeling as a parent so you don't keep them bottled up. Release your inner anxiety and frustrations in a safe and healthy way.

- **Join a new parent group.** Being around other parents who are experiencing what you're going through as a new parent can help ease the emotional load of parenthood and connect you with new people who might become friends.

- **Make grooming appointments.** Does it feel like months since you've gotten a haircut, had your nails done, or gotten a facial? A little pampering can feel like a luxury for Mom and Dad, but spiffing yourself up will give you a lift while you enjoy some cherished time alone.

- **Give yourself small treats during the day.** Maybe it's grabbing your favorite Starbucks beverage, reading a few pages of your book, or enjoying a long hug with your spouse. Pay attention to these little moments and savor them as if they are gifts.

- **Practice a mindful hobby.** When your baby is napping and you don't want to nap yourself, find a hobby that involves just enough focus and challenge to keep your mind engaged. Consider knitting, coloring in an adult coloring book, sketching, playing chess, working a Rubik's Cube, carpentry, flower arranging, beading, origami, or writing. Choose a hobby you can easily put down if your baby needs you.

6. Develop a Short Meditation Habit

Developing a meditation practice is like setting up a savings account that pays increasing dividends for your parenting skills, your well-being, and your child's successful development.

Studies[17] confirm that regular meditation helps you develop emotional equanimity, focus, empathy, and a stronger memory. Physically, it supports your immune system, improves the quality of your sleep, reduces anxiety, and improves heart health.

On a practical level, it helps you better cope with the daily challenges and stressors involved with being a parent. It can also help you and your partner maintain your close connection during this stressful phase of life—especially if you both practice it.

As your child grows old enough to learn how to meditate, help them cultivate the practice in age-appropriate ways. Meditation has been shown[18] to help children improve concentration and attention, make better grades in school, cope better with major stressors, improve overall mental health, regulate emotions, develop empathy, and foster self-awareness.

You may not have time for a long meditation session each day, but even if you squeeze in ten or fifteen minutes, you'll still reap plenty of benefits. Of course, you'll need to plan your meditation time around your baby's nap schedule so you aren't interrupted.

If your partner or a friend is watching your baby while you meditate, try to go outside or to your parked car so you can't

17 https://nccih.nih.gov/health/meditation/overview.htm
18 https://www.forbes.com/sites/alicegwalton/2016/10/18/the-many-benefits
-of-meditation-for-children/#3b7a33d1dbe3

hear your baby cry, which can make you feel anxious and cause letdown in nursing mothers.

Here are the steps for a ten-minute meditation practice, as outlined in our book *10-Minute Mindfulness*:

- Set a timer for ten minutes. Sit in a chair or cross-legged on the floor with a cushion. Keep your spine erect and your hands resting gently in your lap.

- Close your eyes, or keep them open with a downward-focused gaze. Then take a few deep, cleansing breaths.

- Become aware of your breathing. Notice the air moving in and out through your nostrils and the rise and fall of your chest and abdomen (as we explain in the Three Mindful Breaths method). Allow your breaths to come naturally, without forcing them.

- Begin counting your breaths, mentally saying the number as you exhale. Try counting backward from ten, or, instead, think the word "in" as you inhale and "out" as you exhale.

- When your thoughts wander (which they will do a lot in the beginning), gently return to the sensation of breathing. Don't judge yourself or your intrusive thoughts. Just lead your mind back to focused attention on breathing.

- As you breathe, you'll notice other perceptions and sensations, like sounds, physical discomfort, emotions, etc. Simply notice these as they arise in your awareness, and then gently return to your breathing.

- If you observe that you've been lost in thought, view your thoughts as though you are an outside witness with no judgment or emotion. Label them by saying, "There are those intrusive thoughts again." Then return your attention to the breathing.

- Continue with these steps until you are increasingly just a witness to all sounds, sensations, emotions, and thoughts as they arise and pass away.

- As you end your meditation time, take a few more deep, cleansing breaths, open your eyes, and gently continue with your day.

This meditation break is particularly useful in the late afternoon when parents often feel the most exhausted and emotionally spent. If you can get away for a few minutes of meditation, you'll notice you have more bandwidth to get through the evening tasks before you put baby to bed.

7. Learn Mindful Walking

If you don't have time for meditation every day, or you can't get a break to be alone, another alternative is mindful walking—something you can do with your baby.

Most babies enjoy the rocking/bouncing motion of being held and carried or moved in a baby sling or stroller. More importantly, you get a chance to exercise, be outside, and also practice mindfulness at the same time.

Walking meditation is a simple method for reclaiming calm and feeling connected with your baby and yourself. It also gives you both a change of scenery with different sights, smells, and sounds, which can be soothing and stress-relieving.

While some walking meditations can be more formal (like a traditional Buddhist walking meditation[19]), walking with your baby needs to be flexible and less formal.

But any type of walking meditation requires engaging all your senses as you become intentionally aware of your feet hitting the ground, the sights around you, the air you breathe, and sounds you hear. You also want to be aware of your baby and how he feels as you hold him, or how he responds as you push him in the stroller.

If you'd like to try a walking meditation, here's how to practice mindful walking:

- **Anchoring or standing still.** Start by standing in one place, bringing your focus to your weight moving through your

---

19   https://www.insightmeditationcenter.org/books-articles/instructions-for
-walking-meditation/

feet and onto the ground. Make a mental note of all of the subtle movements that happen throughout your body to help keep you balanced in that standing position. Slowly shift your weight from one side to the other, going back and forth and noticing all of the small movements happening in your body.

- **Begin walking.** Notice how your weight moves as you take your first step. Walk as you normally would, but make sure that you are staying at a slow pace. You want to make sure that you don't make any physical changes to how you typically walk, only mental changes.

- **Become aware of your body.** Take some time to focus on each part of your body as you walk. Pay attention to the feelings, from the bottoms of your feet all the way up through the top of your head. If you notice any tension in your body, breathe through the tense areas, mentally sending relaxation through each part.

- **Be mindful of your breathing.** Don't hold your breath while walking, but also try not to breathe too hard because that may indicate that you are walking too quickly. Make sure to take deep breaths while walking at a normal pace.

- **Become aware of the sensations you're having.** Notice everything that is going on in your body, whether it is pleasant or not. Accept these without judgment and just see them for what they are. Take a mental note of everything that goes on throughout your body as you are walking. If you notice things that are going on around you that are either pleasant or unpleasant, allow them to pass you by. Don't let them distract you or take you out of your zone—unless, of course, your baby needs your attention.

- **Notice your thoughts and emotional states.** How are you feeling? Are you relaxed? Content? Anxious or irritated? Maybe you are feeling happy and relieved to be outside on your walk. Just recognize your emotions that come and go during your walk.

  Also, pay attention to what your mind is doing. Is it active or clear? Is it running quickly or taking a rest? Are you thinking about irrelevant things that are taking away from your meditation practice, or are you able to remain focused? Just notice what is going on mentally without any judgment.

- **Shift your focus to your baby.** If you are holding or carrying your baby in a sling, notice how her warm body feels against you and how it feels to carry her weight. If you are pushing a stroller, pay attention to the sensations of walking and pushing.

  Notice your baby's responses to being outside. Is she alert, sleepy, or fussy? Does she seem content and relaxed? What feelings does this time with your baby evoke for you? Reflect on those for a moment.

  You may find yourself irritated if your baby is crying or demands attention while you are trying this walking meditation. Rather than judging the situation, simply shift your attention from the walking meditation to the actions you are taking to tend to your baby.

8. Remember, This Too Shall Pass

Shortly after Barrie had her first child, the cataclysmic realization that life as she knew it was over hit her like a sledgehammer. It dawned on her that for the next eighteen years, she was responsible for another human being and that she had lost the freedom and independence she'd enjoyed before having a baby.

This shocking moment of awareness is especially profound for first-time parents of infants. The 24/7 hands-on care required by a new baby, coupled with sleep deprivation, can feel like a life sentence when you don't know what to expect over the coming days, weeks, and months. Your days blur into nights, your schedule is non-existent, and you worry that you're doing everything wrong.

Now looking back on this time from the perspective of an empty-nester, Barrie can see how brief and wondrous the parenting years were. However, at the time, they felt never-ending.

When you despair at the constant juggling of midnight feedings, colicky screaming, and walking your baby for hours, try to remember this truth: This too shall pass.

Likewise, when your baby is smiling at you, his little body is warm against yours, and your heart is melting with love, remember the same words: This too shall pass.

Instead of feeling resentful or frustrated during the challenging moments, shift your thoughts to the knowledge that it won't be this way forever. Whatever you are dealing with is temporary.

Rather than assuming your little cherub will always be there, smiling and cooing at you, cherish the moment with all the intensity you can muster. Your baby will turn into a teenager before you can blink.

Reminding yourself regularly of the fleeting nature of child-rearing and the importance of each age and stage of your child's development helps keep you grounded in the present moment. There are 6,570 days in your child's first eighteen years of life when he or she is in your care. Make *every* day count!

9. Understand Your Baby's Cries

One of the most challenging parts of parenting an infant is figuring out what he needs when he fusses or cries. Your baby can't tell you with words that he's hungry or needs to walk away from an overstimulating environment. But with a little mindful attention, you can learn to recognize what your baby is trying to communicate.

Often, figuring out those cries is just a matter of trial and error. You try feeding, changing, and rocking your little one until you land on what works. Of course, that can take hours after you start the process, as you may try several options before your baby is calmed.

Eventually, you will learn to recognize what some of his cries are signaling by their sound and intensity—but you *must* pay attention.

In the fog of sleep deprivation and anxiety about what to do to calm your baby, you can forget to really listen to what your baby is trying to tell you. Rather than mindlessly giving her a bottle or assuming she might be cold, take a moment to think about what your baby is doing and how her cries sound to you.

Fortunately, there are some dependable clues to help you figure this out. Understanding different types of baby cries can help you interpret what your own baby might need.

Here are seven types of cries, what they mean, and what you can do for your baby when you hear them:

1. Hunger

A hungry baby might start with whimpering, and then the cry will build and become loud and rhythmic (wah, wah, wah). The individual cries will often be short and low-pitched.

You may also notice your baby rooting around for a breast and trying to suck on his fingers. Try to calm your baby before feeding him so he doesn't choke from sucking milk too quickly and forcefully.

2. Pain

If your baby is in pain, she'll begin to cry suddenly and intensely. It may sound high-pitched, and the cries will be loud, brief, and ear-piercing. Your baby is trying to tell you it's urgent, so if you hear this type of cry, check on your baby immediately and look for the source of the problem (an open diaper pin or pinched finger, for example).

If she's arching her back and her tummy feels hard, it could be gas, so hold and soothe her. Prolonged, intense crying merits a call to the pediatrician.

3. Tiredness or Discomfort

A whiny, nasal-sounding cry that's continuous and builds in intensity is often a sign that he is tired, especially if he's rubbing his eyes, pulling his ears, and yawning. It could also signal that baby needs a diaper change or that he needs to be picked up because he's not comfortable.

4. Overstimulation

A fussy, whiny cry can also signal that your baby feels overstimulated, especially if she's turning her head away from sights or sounds or is pushing away. Take your baby to a quiet place to soothe and calm her.

5. Colic

Colicky cries can make you think your baby is in real distress because they sound like intense wails or even screams. They often occur in the late afternoon or early evening and can last for several hours.

Try putting her in a comforting position, like laying her on her tummy across your knees or on your forearm. The pressure might soothe her stomach and help her release gas.

6. Illness

If your baby is whimpering more than wailing, and the cries are of a lower pitch, he might be sick or feverish. Check your baby for other symptoms like fever, diarrhea, rashes, or vomiting. Call your doctor or on-call nurse to talk about the crying and symptoms.

7. Boredom

Sometimes your baby cries because he is bored and needs a change of scenery or a different toy. He may be cooing happily for a while and then begin to fuss. Try moving him to a different location, taking him for a walk, or offering a new toy that can intrigue him.

You can find YouTube videos like this one[20] that can help you better recognize the sounds of these various cries and how they match your baby's cries.

But remember, the best judge of what your baby needs is you. As you become more aware of the different cries and signals your child is giving you, you'll be able to respond more quickly with exactly what your baby needs. As a result, you'll feel more connected to your baby and more secure as a mindful parent who's in tune with your child.

---

20   https://www.youtube.com/watch?v=9vCPMoILBv0

10. Journal Your Feelings and Your Baby's Milestones

You'll have a thousand things to remember and chronicle with a new baby in the house. You'll want to keep track of:

- Feedings
- Medication doses (for you or baby)
- Number of wet or soiled diapers
- Sleep schedules
- Doctor's appointments
- Food sensitivities (how your diet impacts your baby if you're breastfeeding)
- Gifts you've received for baby

All of these are essential, practical topics to keep in a journal or notebook. It's important to track your baby's schedules and changes so that you have information to share with your pediatrician to make sure your baby is progressing well.

But in the flurry of all the tracking, feeding, rocking, diaper changing, and endless laundry, big and momentous things are happening to you and your baby.

Every day, your baby is changing, growing, and becoming more of a person. The developmental milestones are coming so quickly you can hardly believe how alert and responsive your baby is just by the end of the first month.

You and your partner are undergoing enormous shifts in your lives with all of the accompanying emotions attached to this big change. Mom may feel especially emotional given all of the hormonal changes happening in her body. She may experience some postpartum blues or even depression.

Dad, too, may feel some powerful and unnerving emotions, feeling both overwhelmed and elated by this exciting new adventure.

One of the best ways to process what's going on with you and your baby is through mindful journaling. Not only will journaling about your baby's development and your own feelings help you process and release your emotions, but it will also help you remember all of the intense highs and lows of this surreal time.

Your journal might be a priceless heirloom that you can pass on to your child in later years. And the act of journaling itself is a mindfulness activity that requires focus, intention, and self-awareness.

As we say in our book *Effortless Journaling*,[21] "A journal practice also allows you to start a dialogue within yourself about your inner and outer worlds. It affords clarity where there was none, which is an innate gift of mindfulness. When you pay attention, life becomes pristinely clear."

During a time when your days feel foggy and life seems a bit out of control, journaling can anchor you and help you adjust to your new lives as parents.

You may not have time to write pages and pages in your journal, but jotting down your daily thoughts and feelings (as well as your baby's milestones) is both a mindfulness and self-care practice.

---

21 https://www.amazon.com/Effortless-Journaling-Journal-Endless-Writing -ebook/dp/B07K8WDFPY

There is plenty of evidence[22] that journaling is beneficial for your physical and mental health.

A journaling practice has been shown to:

- Decrease stress and anxiety
- Improve coping skills
- Cultivate feelings of gratitude
- Reduce rumination and negative thinking
- Improve your ability to articulate and clarify your thoughts
- Foster self-awareness
- Improve your immune function
- Improve relationships by fostering a better frame of mind for reconciling with others
- Improve problem-solving
- Enhance your capacity for learning new things

The least expensive and least structured form of journaling is simply using a spiral notebook and pen to track your baby's milestones and chronicle your emotions during these joyful but demanding days.

If you only have a few minutes a day for writing, just jot down a line or two. These brief notations will help you remember the changes you're seeing in your little one and the events of the day that you want to highlight (visits from friends or family, a special moment with your spouse, your feelings about going back to work for the first time, etc.).

---

22   https://positivepsychology.com/benefits-of-journaling/

However, most new parents will either receive as a gift or choose for themselves a special baby book or journal that's a bit more elaborate and special than your basic Dollar Store notebook.

Before you begin a journal or feel obligated to use the one you received as a gift, there are a few things you'll want to consider:

- How much time can you devote to journaling each day? If not much, consider a "one line a day" or bullet-type journal.

- Are you journaling to process your emotions, chronicle your baby's milestones, or track each day's events? Or all of the above? A memory journal gives you the space to write about all of these.

- Do you want your journal to be read by your child one day? Any type of journal will work as long as it's a good-quality journal written with a pen that won't fade over time. You might avoid the spiral notebook and Bic pen.

- Do you prefer to be prompted about what to write or to write whatever you choose? A journal with prompts geared to new parents is perfect if you need some direction for your journaling.

- Do you want to include photos, drawings, cards, and other items in the journal? If so, a scrapbook journal with space to write, as well as pockets and pages for memorabilia, is what you'll need.

- Will you be journaling alone or sharing a journal with your spouse or partner? If you will be sharing, choose a journal specifically for two people, or one that has plenty of room for both of you to write.

Some of our favorite journals and baby books for new parents include:

- One Line A Day: A Five-Year Memory Book:[23] This is an ideal daily journal for busy moms. Forces you to focus on your day's highlights (and low points). Easy to start since it doesn't demand too much time. It also helps you keep track of family activities and revisit past events.

- The Mindfulness Journal: Daily Practices, Writing Prompts, and Reflections for Living in the Present Moment:[24] You can use this journal to incorporate mindfulness into child- and family-rearing. Being a new mom can be overwhelming and exhausting; using *The Mindfulness Journal* can give you the opportunity to take a break and reflect.

- First 5 Years Baby Memory Book + Clean-Touch Ink Pad + Gift Box:[25] If you want to chronicle your baby's milestone, but don't have the time and energy to record every event, this journal pack covers the big milestones and basic details. It also comes with a clean-touch ink pad that you can use to embed your baby's footprints.

- Stories for My Child (Guided Journal): A Mother's Memory Journal:[26] This beautiful journal can be used as a record of milestones and stories you want your child to read about when they grow up. It has inspiring illustrations, prompts, and even a bound-in envelope where you can enclose a letter to give your child when they leave the nest.

23 https://www.amazon.com/One-Line-Day-Five-Year-Journal/dp/0811870197

24 https://www.amazon.com/dp/1973531690

25 https://www.amazon.com/dp/B01N75BOO9

26 https://www.amazon.com/Stories-My-Child-Guided-Journal/dp/1419719858

- Five-Year Memory Journal: 366 Thought-Provoking Prompts to Create Your Own Life Chronicle:[27] A long-term journal to help you track your thoughts, emotions, circumstances, decisions, and how they change over time. Each page has suggestions that help you get started.

- Promptly Journals - Childhood History Journal:[28] An elegant hardbound journal composed of 254 pages that covers every stage of your child's life until eighteen years. There are pages for photos, milestones, family history, and blank pages for special occasions.

- A Year with You: A Keepsake Journal for Two to Share:[29] A great "fill-in-the-blanks" journal for couples in all stages. It's filled with thoughtful prompts and open-ended questions, giving couples some things to think about and bond over.

The infancy and baby stage will be over before you know it, and establishing mindful parenting practices during these early days will help prepare you for the joys and challenges ahead of you.

Let's move on to the toddler stage and explore how you can be a more mindful parent during these magical years in your child's development.

---

27 https://www.amazon.com/Five-Year-Memory-Journal-Thought-Provoking -Chronicle/dp/1454911271

28 https://www.amazon.com/Promptly-Journals-Childhood-Keepsake-Preg nancy/dp/B07DRP3Y56

29 https://www.amazon.com/Year-You-Keepsake-Journal-Share/dp/149263 8390

TODDLERS (AGES 1–3 YEARS)

Just when you think you have this "parenting thing" under control, your child enters the toddler years—nature's not-so-funny way of teaching you that a miniature human with an adorable face is actually running the show.

You're forced to be physically and emotionally present with your child whether you like it or not. And at this stage, being present means being on your toes, chasing, protecting, and practicing endless patience.

This may be the most physically demanding stage of child-rearing. Between your baby's rapid milestone developments (walking, climbing, etc.) and her daily unexpected and seismic emotional outbursts, it may seem your little angel has transformed into the Tasmanian devil—or at least the Energizer Bunny.

Once she is mobile, you are constantly on the go, running after her and trying to stay one step ahead so she doesn't self-destruct. Keeping your little one out of harm's way requires constant vigilance. Even when she's napping you never know when you'll find your toddler climbing over the side of the crib or dangling by her hands, waiting for rescue.

There's so much to learn and explore with her newfound mobility, and everything must be touched and tasted—from bugs to blocks. Your toddler often wants to do things herself, like eating or drinking from a cup, leaving a trail of sticky goo in her wake.

Her developing realization that she's a separate individual means she's going to assert herself and communicate her likes and dislikes in not-so-subtle ways. Your once peaceful home is suddenly punctuated by meltdowns, tantrums, screaming, hitting, throwing, biting, and running away from you. How can this little person wreak so much havoc?

Although your toddler is developing language skills (Noooo! Mine!!!!) to express her ideas, wants, and needs, she doesn't understand logic or have much self-control. This often calls for a near-saintly effort on your part to remain calm and loving to effectively manage the never-ending test of wills between you and your child.

There's no question—mindful parenting in these years may prove more difficult than during the baby days. Your physical and emotional bandwidth will certainly be stretched by potty training, picky eating, and toddler stubbornness.

Naps have gone from two to one per day, and they're getting shorter. You may be getting more sleep, but you have less time to get things done (personal care, laundry, food preparation, and clutter cleanup) because you're on high alert with this highly active little person who has strong opinions and no filters.

Of course, there will be plenty of wonderful moments with your growing baby. Watching her develop a personality, say her first words, and toddle across the room to your waiting arms are unforgettable pleasures. Seeing the wonder in your child's eyes as she discovers a flower or notices her shadow for the first time is thrilling.

Yes, you must be present with your child to gently remove the dirty toy from her mouth, calm her tantrum without anger, or pick her up when she stumbles. But don't forget to be present in those moments as your baby discovers the world around her and begins to share her unique personality with you, her trusted parents.

The toddler years are a great time to introduce mindfulness to your child to help establish a lifelong, beneficial habit. Says writer David Gelles in an article for the *New York Times*:[30]

> Part of the reason why mindfulness is so effective for children can be explained by the way the brain develops. While our brains are constantly developing throughout our lives, connections in the prefrontal circuits are created at their fastest rate during childhood. Mindfulness, which promotes skills that are controlled in the prefrontal cortex, like focus and cognitive control, can therefore have a particular impact on the development of skills including self-regulation, judgment, and patience during childhood.

And, of course, you still want to carve out mindfulness time for yourself so you can recharge and maintain the physical and emotional energy you need to parent effectively.

---

30 https://www.nytimes.com/guides/well/mindfulness-for-children

What to Expect during This Stage

12–18 Months

At this stage, your child is learning to eat with a spoon and is probably spilling a lot. He's also exploring everything he can reach—high and low.

Your child will probably have temper tantrums—especially when he's tired or overwhelmed or when you've thwarted his desires one too many times (or at least once). And if you're taking him to a playdate or to day care, he may cling to you out of fear that you won't come back.

Children at this stage enjoy playing with toys and are often possessive of every toy they see that appeals to them.

Learning to walk usually happens at this stage, though many children begin practicing before the end of their first year. There will still be plenty of falls, and you'll want to clear their domain of fragile objects and furniture with sharp corners.

Your child might also enjoy taking off his shoes and socks—shortly after you put them on or as soon as your back is turned.

18–24 Months

At this stage, your child is moving more quickly around the house—walking more proficiently, possibly even running, and climbing on everything that can be climbed. It's all in the name of exploration, and everything that your toddler can see that he finds interesting is fair game.

He may also be even more possessive—not only with his own toys but with anything he sees that he wants. Saying, "No, that's Christian's toy," makes no sense to him because he feels he has a right to everything he wants.

24–36 Months

Toddlers at this stage may feel empathy and concern toward their fellow toddlers, crying or looking frantic with worry when they see another child upset.

Your toddler will probably want more space to explore his world, so he might not want to hold your hand all the time. He'll still need you to keep a close eye on him, though, because his zest for exploration is greater than his ability to predict the consequences of his actions.

He's also probably stubborn and rigid in his thinking, insisting on having things his way—as if having it any other way were cruel and unusual punishment. On the other hand, he may have developed some fears he didn't have before, such as separation, loud noises, big animals, etc.

What Your Toddler Needs during This Stage

Your toddler needs your unconditional love, cuddles, kisses, and attention. He'll want to hear your voice throughout the day—talking, singing, and reading to him.

He'll want space to explore his world, but he'll need your watchful eye at mealtime, at playtime, and really whenever he's awake and can reach something that might hurt him. Pets and toddlers often don't mix well, so they shouldn't be left alone together.

Your child needs firm limits and consistency from you, as well as heartfelt praise and positive attention. He needs to know you're proud of him and that you delight in his company.

No parent is perfect, and your child will need to hear you apologize when you make a mistake or scare him in some way.

Now let's go over some mindful parenting and mindfulness ideas during the toddler years to help you during this especially busy time.

11. Research This Stage of Development

It's hard to get too upset with a helpless infant who can't move or feed himself, even when he's screaming his little lungs out. You may feel tired or overwhelmed, but angry or irritated—not so much.

The same can't be said during the toddler years. If your toddler were capable of conniving, you'd think she planned her conniption fit for the moment your dinner guests arrive. Or maybe your little guy spilled juice on his new outfit to get back at you for dressing him in such an uncomfortable getup.

Barrie once walked in on her two-year-old daughter "helping" her finish a portrait she was drawing by coloring all over it. It was all Barrie could do to keep her composure and not melt down in tears herself.

You've likely seen parents getting frustrated and angry or even spanking their toddlers over tantrums, defiance, or selfish behavior with other children. We all get triggered when our children embarrass us, don't follow directions, or misbehave. We feel judged by those around us and want to show them that we're good parents and can control our children.

But it's our job as mindful parents to understand experiences through our children's stage of development and adjust our reactions and behaviors accordingly—whether or not someone else is watching.

That's why it's especially important at this stage to recognize that your toddler is a *developing* child who needs gentle discipline, routines, praise, and patience, even with the most trying behaviors.

Anger, corporal punishment, and shaming only evoke fear and hurt feelings for your child, but they don't help him learn internal decision making and acceptable behavior. Redirection of aggressive behaviors is far more useful in helping your child learn prosocial behaviors.

Being firm and consistent about the rules but calm when your child forgets them is essential for your toddler's emotional security and healthy development.

We believe that part of being a mindful parent, especially if you're a first-time parent, is being knowledgeable about the expected behaviors, milestones, fears, and needs of your toddler.

Knowing what to expect, what your child understands, and how to discipline accordingly shows you are being intentional rather than reactionary when it comes to your child. And there are so many resources available to help you educate yourself. Here are a few:

Your Pediatrician

Your child's doctor has probably seen hundreds of children and is intimately familiar with your toddler's developmental stage and what to expect.

Talk to him or her and ask the questions you might feel embarrassed to ask about your child's behavior and how you should manage expectations, discipline, and rules with a one- to three-year-old.

Although there are some typical expectations for this stage (e.g., the terrible twos), not all children are the same. Your pediatrician has observed a large cross-section of toddlers and can give you assurances when your child's behavior is normal and offer help when it's not.

Other Parents

Some of the best resources for parenting your child are other parents. When you have a toddler, nothing feels better than having friends who give you that nod of understanding when your little rascal is acting rascally.

Friends or family members who have gone through the toddler years with their kids can give you real-world feedback on what you're going through and how to handle it.

Experienced parents, especially those who have multiple children, can help you manage your stress with humor and encouragement and offer tips on dealing with typical toddler behavior without losing your cool.

Pay attention to other parents of toddlers, especially those who seem to have it figured out. Don't be embarrassed to ask for advice or ideas on handling a particular problem. Sometimes you need new ideas and fresh thinking if your previous methods have stopped working.

Books

There are thousands of parenting books available from highly acclaimed experts and doctors to help you better understand your toddler and how to manage his behaviors mindfully. The hard part is choosing one or two that work for you.

You might consider getting a book focused specifically on the toddler years so you can narrow your choices. Here are a few we suggest.

- *The Happiest Toddler on the Block: How to Eliminate Tantrums and Raise a Patient, Respectful, and Cooperative One- to Four-Year-Old*

- *Toddler Discipline for Every Age and Stage: Effective Strategies to Tame Tantrums, Overcome Challenges, and Help Your Child Grow*

- *How Toddlers Thrive: What Parents Can Do Today for Children Ages 2–5 to Plant the Seeds of Lifelong Success*

- *Toddler 411: Clear Answers and Smart Advice for Your Toddler*

- *How to Talk so Little Kids Will Listen: A Survival Guide to Life with Children Ages 2–7*

- *What to Expect the Second Year: From 12 to 24 Months*

Parenting Blogs

You could spend all day perusing the helpful parenting blogs you'll find online. You'll find some spot-on tips and just-in-time reassurance from many of the mommy (and daddy) bloggers who are going through exactly what you are going through. We like the ones who are committed to parenting mindfully, just like you.

Feel free to check out:

- Messy Motherhood,[31] a "guilt-free, judgment-free zone where we can be real about the messiness of motherhood." Written by Amanda Rueter, a children's mental health counselor and mom of two boys.

---

31 https://messymotherhood.com

- Aha! Parenting[32] helps parents of kids from babies through teens "create a more peaceful home – and happy, responsible, considerate kids." Founded by Dr. Laura Markham, who trained as a Clinical Psychologist at Columbia University and is the author of the "Peaceful Parent" books.

- Feed the Parent[33] promotes "a calm, connected, conscious style of parenting" that uses mindfulness and meditation. Founder Suzie Brown is a mindful parenting coach and mother and she writes about difficult behavior, emotions, kids cooperation, everyday mindfulness, sleep, and technology.

- A Mother Far from Home[34] is for parents who "love the parenting, but hate the chaos." Founder Rachel Norman is a baby sleep, routine, and family life consultant and a mother of four; she teaches parents "mindsets, routines, and habits that take the chaos out of parenting."

- The Parenting Junkie[35] is written by Avital Schreiber Levy, a Childhood Designer who believes that "parents deserve an integrated parenting philosophy – not a one-size-fits all dogma."

- Happily Family[36] is run by couple Cecilia and Jason Hilkey, preschool teachers who now help parents "communicate with their kids to avoid meltdowns and power struggles" through parenting classes, parent coaching, and virtual parenting conferences.

32   https://www.ahaparenting.com/about
33   https://www.feedtheparent.com/about
34   https://amotherfarfromhome.com/about/
35   https://www.theparentingjunkie.com/about/
36   https://www.happilyfamily.com/about/

- Positive Parenting Solutions[37] is all about equipping "parents with the tools they need to get kids to listen without nagging, yelling or losing control" by using positive parenting strategies. Founder Amy McCready is certified in Positive Discipline; she began teaching her parenting methods in 2004 and launched the online course in 2008.

Choose two or three trusted resources to educate yourself about your toddler's needs and behaviors so that you're better aware of how to best guide your child without too much frustration for you or her.

---

37   https://www.positiveparentingsolutions.com/about-us

12. Start Your Day Calmly

Once your little bundle of energy wakes up in the morning, you'll hit the ground running—and if your toddler serves as your alarm clock, that means you're starting your day on high alert. When you're frazzled and agitated by 8:00 a.m., it's hard to reclaim that inner reservoir of calm to handle all of the demands of your day.

Hopefully, you're getting better sleep than you did during the infant and baby stages. If so, consider waking up thirty minutes before you're officially "on" so you can begin your day with a calm frame of mind.

This is especially important if you're also tending to other children or heading out to work in the morning. Thirty minutes less sleep is worth the positive benefits of giving yourself that buffer.

So what should you do with that thirty minutes of time in the morning? Nothing. Or mostly nothing. Use this time to peacefully transition from sleep to activity in a slow and calm manner.

During this time, you could...

- Meditate
- Pray
- Write in your journal
- Visualize your day
- Repeat positive affirmations
- Do some light stretching
- Take a bath

- Read something inspirational
- Make love with your spouse or partner

On the other hand, don't use this time to...

- Watch the news
- Get on social media
- Check your phone or email
- Worry about the day ahead
- Do chores
- Address conflict or controversial topics with your spouse

You will be doing yourself and your child a huge favor by starting your morning with a surplus of peaceful energy. It will allow you to be more available to your little one as you greet him for a new day. And you'll feel better about yourself as a calm and centered parent who isn't racing around mindlessly.

13. Become an Expert at Toddler Tantrums

Having that surplus of peaceful energy will serve you well during the toddler phase, as you'll often need all the inner calmness you can muster. As your child grows from infancy to toddlerhood, that sweet little baby gets *very, very* opinionated about what he or she wants.

And if your toddler doesn't like your response, you'll find yourself facing off with a tiny person who suddenly has superhuman lung strength and the ability to make a scene of epic proportions, often in public places where all eyes are boring in on you. Toddler tantrums are enough to fill the most mindful, centered parent with an inexplicable sense of rage and mortification.

Whether you call it the "terrible twos" or the "terrible threes," when your child reaches this volatile phase, you'll likely experience a weekly routine peppered with meltdowns. According to research reported in Nelson Essentials of Pediatrics[38] (6th edition, 2010), in U.S. studies, "50% to 80% of 2- to 3-year-old children have had regular tantrums, and 20% are reported to have daily tantrums. The behavior appears to peak late in the third year of life."

Steve's son is currently at this stage where an emotional explosion can be triggered by just about any enforced rule or request. Just saying "No" in a calm voice can lead to a writhing-on-the-floor conniption.

Despite the way they trigger adults, tantrums are a perfectly natural part of your children's development, and you'll do yourself a favor to better understand the purpose of these inconvenient and maddening hissy fits.

---

38 https://www.amazon.com/Essentials-Pediatrics-Marcdante-Kliegman-Behrman/dp/B004LWL0QG

Your toddler isn't trying to drive you crazy or embarrass you. They aren't capable of reasoning and manipulating—yet. (Older toddlers can figure out how to use tantrums to get their way.)

Toddlerhood is a time in children's lives when their feelings are very intense and overwhelming, and they haven't developed emotional regulation. Tantrums are a result of their needs and desires being thwarted by you or by their own limitations and inabilities. And some children have inborn temperament traits that make them more prone to tantrums.

Tantrums are often the aftershocks of their growing independence from you crashing into your boundaries for them (established for their safety and proper socialization). Toddlers simply don't have the vocabulary to express the tumult and disequilibrium of their inner worlds. Without words, how else can they communicate how angry, sad, or frustrated they're feeling?

In fact, tantrums serve a real purpose in your child's social and emotional development. According to Margot Sunderland in her book, *The Science of Parenting*, toddlers have tantrums because "the emotional regulation of a child's feelings during storms of feelings enables them to establish essential brain pathways for managing stress and being assertive in later life."

Here's what the authors at the Parenting for the Brain site[39] have to say about the science of tantrums:

> When a toddler is overcome by stress such as rage, a little alarm (amygdala) inside his emotional brain (a.k.a. limbic or lower brain) is triggered. This alarm is mature at birth because an infant needs to be able to sense distress and

---

39 https://www.parentingforbrain.com/deal-toddler-temper-tantrums/

signal to his parents, usually by crying, to survive. On the other hand, a child's local brain (a.k.a. prefrontal cortex or higher brain) is not sufficiently developed to manage that alarm system.

When this happens, stress hormones are released to course through the toddler's body and emotions become intense. This hormonal storm causes anguish and emotional pain, which amounts to physical pain. The stress hormones also hinder the toddler's ability to access the rational thinking inside his logical brain. Essentially, the toddler is having a "brain freeze."

Knowing that tantrums are a normal part of toddler development can make them less dismaying for you, especially if you understand what triggers them and how to respond. There are different types of tantrums your toddler may display, and recognizing the type (and the trigger) can help you manage the situation more mindfully.

Frustration or Fatigue Tantrums

Toddlers can have temper outbursts when they are frustrated with themselves because they are unable to do or accomplish something, or if they are unable communicate in a way to make you understand them.

Nothing is more frustrating than asking Mommy or Daddy something and getting an unrelated reply—or a helpless stare saying, "I don't understand you."

When your toddler is tired (maybe having missed a nap or awakened too early), she is more prone to reacting emotionally to frustrations.

With frustration or fatigue, your child needs your understanding, support, and help rather than a consequence. If she can't do something she's trying to do, offer your help or praise her for what she has accomplished. Or steer her to another task instead.

If your child is tired, move bedtime up or put her down for a nap if it isn't too close to bedtime. Or give your child something quiet and soothing to do like reading together or doing some deep breathing if she is calm enough.

Demanding and Attention-Seeking Tantrums

Your toddler is frustrated that he isn't getting his way, so a tantrum ensues. For example, you say no to the cookie before dinner or don't allow him to drink from a glass instead of a sippy cup.

Sometimes your toddler is seeking your attention (or the attention of others) by having a meltdown or behaving badly. Whining, stomping feet, slamming doors, and breath-holding are examples of attention-seeking tantrum behaviors.

It's best to ignore these types of tantrums if they aren't too disruptive, or try to shift your toddler's attention to something else. Move to a different room if the tantrum continues to show your child that he doesn't have an audience. Trying to reason with your child is pointless, so allow him to cool off and then be friendly and return to normal.

Disruptive Tantrums

All tantrums feel disruptive, but here we're talking about the meltdowns that prevent you from doing anything except deal with the tantrum. Your child might be hitting you, clinging to you during the outburst, throwing things, or having the tantrum in public.

Putting your child in his or her room or time-out for a few minutes (if at home) or removing your child from a public setting (if out) gives your child the opportunity to calm down, regain control, and reengage with a loving hug from you.

Rage or Out-of-Control Tantrums

Sometimes a toddler's emotions can get so out-of-control that it scares him and you. He might bang his head on the floor, scream wildly, or do something that might cause self-injury.

The best thing you can do during these types of tantrums is hold your toddler, acknowledge his anger, and comfort him until you feel his body start to relax.

For all tantrums...

- Try to catch them when they are small. If you see frustration building, step in with an offer of help or distraction.

- Validate your child's needs and feelings even when they are expressed in emotional outbursts. (More on this in the next section.)

- Take a deep breath and try to stay calm. Your child needs your calm and secure presence.

- Give your child plenty of physical activity to expend some of the stress and frustration that can build up.

- Teach your child how to use his words by teaching him feeling words for the emotions he's experiencing.

- Pick your battles and give your child a way out of the tantrum if the situation isn't worth fighting over.

- Ignore tantrums that aren't disruptive or harmful, redirect when possible, and employ time-outs when necessary. Always prioritize your child's safety.

Now let's dig a little deeper to discuss more ways you can be a mindful parent when it comes to your toddler's behavior and how you want to respond to it. The next three sections will help you be the kind of parent you want to be during some of the most stressful and button-pushing times with your child.

14. Empathize with Your Child's Frustrations

A fundamental part of mindfulness is empathy—the ability to experience and understand another person's thoughts, feelings, and situation from his or her point of view, rather than from your own. And who better to practice empathy with than your own child who needs an advocate and interpreter for her underlying emotions!

But in the heat of a stressful moment for your toddler, it can be hard to relate to her frustrations and feel empathy for them. All you want is for the whining, screaming, hitting, biting, or other aggressive behaviors to stop. Your blood pressure is rising and your mind is laser-focused on the quickest way to ease your own suffering or embarrassment.

Before the next emotion-filled moment like this occurs, take some time to consider your toddler's inner world and how her little-person limitations impact her. Use empathy to view these situations through her eyes.

Imagine how it might feel if...

- You can't articulate your needs and wants.
- The decision-makers around you can't understand you when you try to communicate with them.
- You have little control over your environment, where you go, and what you do.
- You want something really badly, you grab it, and then it's immediately taken away from you.
- You're in the middle of something you enjoy and you're forced to stop.

- Your feelings are hurt, but the big people around you don't seem to understand.

- You want to do something (eat with a fork, drink from a cup, climb on something), but you don't have the bodily control to manage it.

- You try to do something, but a bigger, stronger person prevents you from doing it (even if it's for your own good).

- You're super tired, but you don't know you need sleep and you resist it, making you feel even worse.

- You're happy and having fun, but someone forces you to get into bed and go to sleep.

- You hate mushy peas, green beans, or carrots, but a big person keeps feeding them to you.

A toddler understands enough to recognize he has limitations and that these limitations are thwarting his desires, making him feel sad, and frustrating his sensibilities. You would want to scream, cry, hit, and throw things too if you were faced with these limitations and unable to understand them.

Your child depends on you to interpret these frustrations and feelings and to help make sense of them. He needs you to try your best to walk in his little shoes, to see how maddening the world can be, and to validate and accept his need to express these feelings—even aggressively—because that's often his only option.

He also needs you to soothe him and offer options or distractions. He needs to feel that you, his safe and steadfast person, are there to make it all better.

In these stressful moments, rather than yanking your child away in embarrassment, fussing at him, spanking, or shaming him, you might...

- Draw a mental bubble around you and your toddler so that the only things you're focused on are your child, his feelings, and his well-being—not the others around you.

- Take a breath and remind yourself that your child is trying to tell you something the best way he knows how. You are the adult and can apply emotional self-control. Your child can't.

- Ask yourself, "What is my little one feeling? What does he want to say but cannot?"

- Acknowledge your child's feelings by using a calm and soothing voice and saying something like, "I know you must be really mad." He may not comprehend your words, but he gets your tone. Strive to be a calm presence with him, even as he is in the midst of a full-throated tantrum.

- Remove, redirect, or distract your toddler once he is calmer. For older toddlers, talk about your rules in clear and simple language: "Hitting is not okay. Use your words or we will have to go home."

- Pay attention to clues that reveal the triggers for your child's frustrations or outbursts so that you can try to avoid these situations or manage them in the future.

- Offer positive feedback when your child is expressing himself or dealing with his frustration in appropriate ways. "I liked the way you shared your toy with Taylor. I know it's hard to share."

It's a balancing act between empathizing with your child's underlying emotions and socializing him appropriately, especially in public situations or around other children. You do have to be mindful and considerate of the people around you and the safety of other kids.

But whenever possible, lead with empathy in these flustering moments with your toddler. Let him know that you understand, that you love him, and that you want to comfort him before you distract or discipline. Even angry adults want to feel understood and heard.

15. Use the STOP Method for Mindful Responses

No matter how empathetic you try to be with your toddler, there will be times when empathy evades you. You're so tired, frustrated, or overwhelmed that *you* need a mom or dad to swoop in and save you from a temper tantrum when your toddler has one.

Losing your cool with your toddler and yelling, spanking, or using unnecessary force is not your goal in any situation. You want to bring your most emotionally mature, best self to any interaction with your child—not your reactive self.

As bigger, stronger, socialized adults, we must find ways to manage our exasperation without resorting to behaviors that are upsetting for our little people.

In addition, your toddler is a keen observer, soaking up the way you respond to all situations. If you frequently resort to anger and aggression, so will your child. He's mimicking you, after all, and you want to be a positive role model for your child and his emotional development.

For these reasons, you need a simple way to pause and reset whenever you're feeling a surge of emotions—before you say or do something you regret. You can do this by using the STOP method, an approach you can use through all stages of your child's development.

Here are the steps:

S-Stop — When you are in a stressful situation with your child, or whenever you notice anxiety or stress, stop and pause before you say or do anything.

T-Take a breath — Transfer your awareness from the situation at hand to your breathing. Take a deep, cleansing breath and exhale slowly. Focus on the sensations of the breathing with your full attention.

Also, notice how your mind and body begin to relax, bringing more clarity and releasing tension. When we are in stressful situations, it's difficult to think clearly or perceive any situation accurately.

Awareness of your breathing integrates the cardiovascular system in the body and calms the "fight or flight" areas in the more primitive parts of the brain.

O-Observe — Observe how your focused breathing begins to balance the systems of the body. Notice these calmer feelings. Look at the situation with deeper understanding and, if possible, with empathy. What is really happening with your child in this moment?

P-Proceed — Now that you are in a mindfully responsive state, you can take action that is more loving and appropriate for your child and the situation you are dealing with.

16. Practice Mindful Discipline

It might seem that discipline in the toddler years is more about controlling yourself than it is gaining compliance from your child. Your main goals with discipline at this stage are related to managing behavior and keeping your child safe while beginning the process of teaching your child acceptable behavior. This should all be done in the context of understanding the emotional and cognitive limitations of your toddler.

That being said, there will be times when calming and redirecting aren't enough. You will need to let your child know what is and isn't acceptable and that there are age-appropriate consequences for certain behaviors. The most important part of a mindful discipline plan for your toddler is forethought and consistency.

Use Forethought

Mindful parenting means being deliberate and intentional about your rules and the consequences for breaking those rules. Consider well in advance of potential misbehavior what your non-negotiable dos and don'ts will be and consistently follow through with your predetermined consequences.

You would likely find these behaviors worthy of a consequence if calming and redirecting don't work:

- Having a tantrum in a public place.
- Hitting or otherwise harming another person or animal.
- Doing something dangerous.
- Taking another child's toy.

- Throwing or breaking things.

- Refusing to cooperate with you (putting on clothes, walking out the door, etc.).

- Playing with or touching something breakable or valuable.

Once you know your non-negotiables, plan ahead for consequences to the behaviors so you're not stuck in a tense moment wondering how to respond. The consequences should happen as soon as possible after the infraction, as your toddler won't remember a misbehavior that happened yesterday when you punish him today.

Also, make sure the consequence fits the misbehavior. Canceling a future playdate because your toddler threw food at you won't make sense to him. But he will see a connection if you take away his food and remove him from the high chair, as you calmly explain, "You can't throw your food. Food is for eating."

If your child is having a public tantrum and your efforts at comforting and calming aren't working, then the consequence might be removing him for a time-out. If he is hitting another child or hitting you and you've asked him to stop, hold his hands together and say firmly, "I told you no more hitting, so now we are going home."

Practice Consistency

Consequences for your non-negotiables should happen quickly and consistently—even if others are watching, it's inconvenient, or you'd rather just give another warning. For your toddler (and for all kids and adults), actions speak louder than words, and actions should occur after one warning.

If you aren't consistent with your consequences, you're sending your child mixed messages and teaching her you don't always mean what you say, giving her an opening to practice the misbehavior again.

You can't cave because you don't want to make a scene in front of others or disappoint them. Being a mindful parent requires that you prioritize your child's socialization over your own.

Being consistent is one of the most difficult parts of mindful parenting because it takes commitment and self-discipline. It is easier sometimes to ignore behavior, give in, use warnings without action, make excuses for your child's actions, or delay a consequence until a time that's more convenient for you.

But if you remain committed to teaching your child appropriate behaviors with consistent follow-through when he is young, you'll find he is more responsive to your boundaries and rules as he gets older. It will save you time and energy in later years when your child may test you in more difficult ways.

Pick Your Battles

There will be times when you have to decide whether or not it's worth it to put a stake in the ground over a battle of the wills with your child. For example, you may not want to put up a fight if your child wants to wear a ragged princess costume every day, even if it's driving you crazy.

You might even be inconsistent with your rules around this, allowing her to wear it every day except on certain occasions. Try to be as clear as you can on this inconsistency, and use negotiation and rewards to work around potential conflict. "You can put on your princess dress as soon as we get home from Grandma's" or "You can't wear the princess dress to church today, but you can wear the crown."

There also may be situations in which disciplining your child creates more havoc than it's worth in the moment. Barrie once had her toddler in the pediatrician's office with her while the doctor was examining her older child. Her toddler was misbehaving, but the doctor was in a hurry and trying to communicate information, so she let the behavior go.

There will be times when the needs of those around you trump your need to follow through on a consequence. You may not be able to remove your child from a situation (if you're on an airplane, for example), and you don't want to create a scene that will cause others to suffer. Use distraction and redirection to manage these situations as best you can.

Make Use of Time-Outs

Time-outs work well for preschoolers and older children, but even toddlers can learn from time-outs, especially if they are used appropriately and without anger. A time-out allows your toddler to calm down and removes him from attention and distractions.

You can use a time-out just about anywhere, but you may need to get a little creative when you're away from home. If you have your car with you, you can always use the car seat or pack a small chair or stool to keep in the car when you need it.

This time alone shows your toddler that misbehaving doesn't result in getting his way but rather separates him from fun and play for a short time. It also gives you a few minutes to calm down and stay true to your parenting values without saying or doing something you'll regret later.

Before using a time-out, explain it to your child in a moment when he or she isn't misbehaving. Talk about the behaviors that merit a time-out and how long time-out will last. Practice a "pretend" time-out so your child will know the steps when a real one occurs.

With young toddlers, use time-outs for two or three of the non-negotiable misbehaviors. As your child understands what the misbehaviors are and that you intend to follow through on the consequence, you can use time-outs for additional misdeeds.

The rule of thumb for time-outs is one minute for every year your child is alive. So a two-year-old would sit in time-out for two quiet minutes. The two minutes don't include time whining, getting up, or otherwise making a scene.

Don't begin the time-out until your child is sitting (or standing) quietly. If your child gets up, calmly lead him back to the chair and start over (as many times as necessary).

You may need to stand next to your toddler and let him know that when he sits quietly without leaving the chair, the time-out is over. Using a timer with a bell can help your child wait it out. Some children will fidget, sing, or have quiet sniffling during time-out, which should still count as part of the quiet time.

Once you have implemented a time-out, say nothing—at all. Don't engage with any misbehavior, as your child is trying to get a reaction from you. Don't argue, negotiate, or spank. Even if your child gets up, lead him back to time-out without saying anything.

When time-out is over, ask your toddler if he is ready to get up. If he nods or says yes politely, give him a hug and lead him back to what he was doing or to another activity.

Give Your Child Choices

Sometimes the best defense with your toddler is a good offense. Rather than setting yourself up for the inevitable battle of the wills, give your toddler a choice to deflect his attention away from something he may or may not want to do.

"Would you rather put the blocks away first or the soldiers?"

"Do you want to put on your coat first or your shoes?"

Offering a choice lets your toddler feel as if he's in control of the situation and removes the knee-jerk response of "Noooo! I don't want to!" Just be sure you offer only two choices at any one time. Too many options can be confusing and overwhelming.

If the choice strategy doesn't work on the first try, you might say something like, "Do you want to choose, or do you want Daddy to choose? Shoes or coat?"

It does take more time and patience to offer an option rather than just forcing the situation, but by giving your child some leeway, you are helping him make decisions while keeping his dignity intact.

You are also showing your child that even though you are the adult decision-maker and caregiver, he has some control and decision-making power in his little life. Offering autonomy where you can helps your child build confidence within the secure confines of your loving boundaries.

Pay Attention to Transitions

Toddlers have a particularly hard time moving easily from one activity to another and from one part of a day to another. These transition times are ripe for emotional meltdowns and resistance from your toddler. But knowing this, you can be more mindful about how you handle these transitions so you don't trigger unnecessary misbehavior.

Give your child fair warning that a change is about to occur so that she is prepared for the next activity.

"As soon as Sesame Street is over, we will turn off the TV and eat lunch. I made your favorite pasta."

"After you put three more blocks on your tower, it will be time to put the blocks away and go for a walk. Let's count the blocks together."

"We are going to bed in fifteen minutes, so you only have a little more time to play with your trucks."

The more predictable your daily routine is, the easier these transitions will be for your little one who feels more secure having a sense of what comes next after each activity.

Tailor Discipline to Your Child

There are as many ways to discipline your child as there are misbehaviors. Many child-rearing experts and gurus suggest that there's only one way to get it right and that their approach to discipline applies to all children.

In some situations, this may be true. But often, you are the best judge of the right way to discipline your child to get the desired results.

Some children are more sensitive, tender-hearted, and compliant than others. A stern look or firm word is enough to change the behavior and make a course correction. Other children want to test all of your boundaries before they are ready to comply and follow the rules.

Through trial and error, you'll figure out what it takes to teach your child your expectations and the consequences of not meeting them. You'll see what works well and what doesn't.

Even then, you may need to alter your approach as your child develops. The more you pay attention to your child and his reactions, the better you'll be at creating a discipline plan that works for both of you.

Remember, for toddlers, redirection and distraction (with a warning about your expectations) should be your first option before you employ a consequence. But if you do need to discipline your child, act quickly and consistently to help your child learn and follow your rules.

17. See the World through Your Toddler's Eyes

One of the most delightful qualities of toddlers is their sense of wonder and excitement as they explore the world around them. Everything is new and remarkable—from the clouds in the sky to the muddy puddles they want to jump and splash in.

As adults, we take so many of these simple pleasures and miraculous occurrences for granted. We neglect to pause and notice the possibilities for discovery all around us. We don't foster a learning mindset or arouse our curiosity enough to ask the questions of ourselves that our little ones are always asking us ("Why is the moon so big?" "How do birds fly?").

When you strive to see the world through your toddler's eyes, you'll discover two positive outcomes:

1. You take more time with your child to share in the wonder, joy, and curiosity he experiences every day while helping him learn about the world around him.

2. You become more mindful of the world yourself and continue to learn as you experience again the delight you once had as a child.

So how can you take advantage of these benefits by looking through the lens of your toddler's worldview? Consider these ideas.

FOR YOUR TODDLER...

Slow down and be fully present when your toddler notices something. Observe what she's focused on, squat down next to her, and take notice along with her. Allow your child this moment of curiosity or wonder without rushing or distracting her. Put down your phone, pay attention, and be there with your little person in these moments.

Increase your child's vocabulary by verbally identifying what she is looking at, sensing, or paying attention to.

"That's a daffodil."

"That was a horn honking."

"That lemon tastes sour."

Point out things that you see, hear, smell, or feel, and put names to them.

Put the experiences into context for your child by clarifying the associated emotion or offering an adjective or adverb to describe it.

"Was that big dog scary?"

"Those flowers are so pretty."

"Playing in the sprinkler is fun, isn't it?"

"Ice cream makes me happy."

Explain to your child what she is seeing or experiencing, even if she can't quite comprehend it fully. Your explanations need to be simple and logical for a toddler's limited comprehension.

"That's your shadow. When you stand in front of the sun, you block the sunshine and that makes a shadow."

"Look at that bird's nest. That's where a mama bird takes care of her babies."

Help your child understand (and put into words) any negative or upsetting feelings associated with exploration.

"It's sad to see that the squirrel was hurt by the car."

"Putting gum in your hands feels yucky, doesn't it?"

"It's frustrating when you can't climb like the big boys."

Allow your child to get dirty and messy. Part of exploring and understanding the world requires touching, jumping, and rolling around in it. If you're always pulling your toddler back for fear she'll get dirty, you're depriving her of fun and a learning opportunity.

Answer your child's questions, even if they are endless. Your toddler is longing to understand the world, and you are her main source of information right now. Fortunately, parents today have quick access to any answers they don't know or can't remember by using their smartphones. You don't have to guess at why the moon looks so big or why frogs are slimy—you can look it up at the touch of a button.

Allow your child to talk to people (under your watchful eye)— even safe strangers. Unless your toddler is going through a shy or insecure phase, she wants to meet new friends—and everyone is a potential friend. Let her talk to people in the grocery store line or at the playground if it's clear she isn't bothering them. This is how she learns to socialize with different types of people.

Be positive about safe, new experiences for your child. Meeting your neighbor's big, friendly dog might seem scary, but show your child that it's okay to safely pet the dog. Climbing the ladder to the slide feels daunting for your little one, but reassure her she can do it and that you're right there for her. Let your child know when new experiences are safe, positive, and fun.

Give your child the tools to explore and create. A shovel and pail can provide hours of entertainment and discovery. Finger paints and a big pad on an easel allows your toddler to explore so many senses. Toddler-sized instruments help your child learn about sounds and cause and effect. Be sure your toddler has indoor and outdoor toys and tools for discovery and fun.

FOR YOURSELF...

Pay more attention to the world around you for your own benefit and your child's. When you are taking a stroll with him, point out interesting or beautiful things to your child. Use all your senses to be attentive to the large and small things going on around you, and you'll have a richer experience with your child.

Turn your chores into mindfulness activities for you and your child. Let your toddler stand next to you on a stool as you wash dishes or stir the pot of soup. Give him a shovel to help you plant flowers. Let him soap up the dirty dog when you give it a bath. These might be chores for you, but they are fun, new experiences for your toddler. And with some mindfulness, they will be more enjoyable and positive for you as well.

Seek to understand the emotions that new experiences evoke for your child. A pinecone in the yard seems innocuous to you, but your toddler might find it frightening. A summer rain will send you indoors, but your child finds delight in running around in it. You might be disgusted at the worms your child has dug up, but he thinks they are the coolest things ever. Let your child know that you feel what he feels or at least that you recognize what he is feeling.

Be aware that so many experiences are firsts for your child. Most everything you see and do is old hat for you. But for your little one, the world is a brand-new, exciting, and sometimes scary place. Try to keep that in mind everywhere you go—riding in the car, going to the store, taking a walk outside, or visiting a new friend. Watch your child and try to discern what he is thinking, feeling, or wondering. Ask him questions about his observations.

When you're alone, take the time to savor the little things. Yes, you are in the busiest time of your life and you feel you have to rush from one thing to the next. But become a toddler yourself every now and then by giving yourself permission to enjoy the little things you take for granted. Sit still and enjoy the sunshine, stop and smell a flower, or notice the clouds floating by. Remember what it's like to find pleasure in these neglected little experiences.

18. Create Predictable Routines

Whether or not you're a naturally organized person, having structure in your life can pave the way for more mindfulness and intention in everything you do. As an adult and busy parent, you need routines to stay on task (and move your child peaceably through the day) without the added stress required to figure it out "on the fly."

As you establish your daily routines, do so with intention, prioritizing what is most important or valuable to you. Just setting routines is a mindfulness activity because you're required to carefully consider and plan the structure that guides your life and your child's.

Routines make you more efficient because they reduce the number of decisions you make in a day, freeing you to be present with the activity at hand. They also reduce the need for willpower, which requires focus and mental energy, because each action or behavior has become automatic.

When you have a predictable series of habits or actions, you don't have to expend energy thinking about what to do next. You just do it, almost effortlessly.

This saves you time that can be devoted to your child, your self-care, your spouse or partner, or your other important values. Of course, as the parent of a toddler, many of your routines will be established around your child and her need for structure.

For your toddler, routines and predictability are essential to development. They give her some sense of control, security, and emotional stability, allowing her to explore and learn within the safe confines of the boundaries that you establish for her.

This structure helps her learn to trust the caring adults around her to provide what she needs so she can focus without anxiety on her own mindful tasks of play and discovery.

Routine also helps develop your toddler's prefrontal cortex, the planning and executive functioning part of the brain. It gives your child a sense of time and patterns that are essential to family life—and for life at school and work as she grows.

Toddlers in the twenty-four- to thirty-six-month age range recognize that there are "rules" to life and crave for things to be "just so." Your little one might insist on wearing the same Spiderman mask every day or having you read every word of a favorite book without skipping a part—because that's the way it's supposed to be.

Following these rules and routines gives order to her world—and breaking them feels disorienting and upsetting.

Older toddlers may not need this rigid adherence to sameness, but as they begin to recognize their limitations as small people, they need routine to feel secure even as they start to test their limits.

When your toddler can anticipate what comes next, she becomes more confident and compliant, reducing the number of behavior corrections and power struggles you'll face as a parent.

Some routines and habits are essential for your child's health and safety, like washing hands and brushing teeth. Other routines like greeting people, taking turns, and sharing teach your child important social and language skills.

And since transitions are so challenging for toddlers, routines can help ease your little one from one activity to another without as much frustration or angst.

For both you and your toddler, routines provide precious moments of connection that solidify your bond as parent and child. They compel you to slow down and experience the moment with your toddler without being distracted by "what's next on the list."

Let's review some routines both for you and your toddler that will encourage mindfulness and mindful parenting.

FOR YOU...

Take time to plan routines you want to establish.

Don't allow routines to establish themselves. Set aside a specific time to do this, and be proactive with your plans. Sit down with your spouse or partner (even if he or she isn't the primary caregiver) and discuss the routines you want to develop for yourselves, your family, and your child.

Be intentional and thoughtful about these routines, why you want to establish them, and how they will benefit you and your child. Try to connect them to your family values. Then write down your daily routines and schedule and post the schedule so you remember the routines you want to create.

Having routines doesn't mean you can't break them from time to time, but you'll be grateful to have this structure in place to make your lives calmer, simpler, and more intentional.

Develop your personal morning routine.

Your own morning routine sets the tone for the entire day and can help you reduce stress and stay on track with the rest of your schedule with your child. Try to wake up before your toddler so that you can build some positive momentum, energy, and inner peace to start your day.

We recommend that your morning routine include some kind of mindfulness activity—meditation, breathing, yoga, or simply sipping your tea slowly and mindfully. Your morning routine might also include saying some affirmations, writing in a journal, exercising, or reading something inspirational.

Whatever you include in your morning routine, be sure that it doesn't cause you stress or anxiety. This may be a difficult charge if you're a working parent who has to get out the door by 7:00 a.m. to take your child to day care.

If you only have a few minutes to yourself in the morning, even a quick breathing practice while you're in the shower can help center you. Do your best to plan ahead (packing lunches, getting clothes ready, etc.) so your mornings are as calm and predictable as possible—for you and your child.

Turn some of your routines into rituals.

All routines are not created equal—some should be treated more sacredly than others. Family rituals are routines that are symbolically meaningful and help establish a sense of identity and belonging for all of you. For your child, they can feel comforting, positive, and even fun.

Eating dinner together is one routine that you can turn into a ritual. Rather than strapping your child in the high chair and giving her a bowl of mac and cheese while you wolf down a sandwich, make the dinner hour a peaceful family affair.

- Pull the high chair to the table (or use a booster seat in a real chair).
- Dim the lights and light some candles.
- Put on soft music.
- Ask your child to participate by putting a fork and napkin at each place setting.
- Say a family prayer or mantra of gratitude together. ("I am thankful for this food, I am thankful for my family, and I am thankful for my home.")
- Talk about what you each did during the day.
- Blow out the candles and clear the dishes together.

Other routines, like bath time, story time, or even cleaning up toys, can become ritualized to make them more meaningful and fun. Just thinking about your routines with your child as rituals can make them feel less like tasks and inspire you to approach them creatively.

Your daily routines with your child *can be* monotonous because, let's face it, you're an adult who needs more mental stimulation. But you *do* have a choice. Rather than mechanically plodding through your daily routine with resentment or boredom, try to celebrate each little segment of it with gratitude and joy.

Prioritize naps and bedtimes for everyone.

As you plan your daily routines for yourself and your child, prioritize sleep and rest at the top of your schedule. Good sleep is as important to your family's health and well-being as healthy eating and exercise. For your child, it may be the most important part of his routine.

Numerous studies[40] show that a consistent, healthy sleep routine (between seven and nine hours a night for adults) can:

- Keep your heart healthy by protecting against heart disease and stroke.
- Lower the risk of breast and colon cancer.
- Help prevent stress and high blood pressure.
- Make you more alert and energetic.
- Improve your memory.
- Reduce weight by balancing the hormones that affect weight.
- Reduce the risk of depression.
- Help the body repair itself, as your cells produce more protein while you sleep.

Toddlers generally need twelve to fourteen hours of sleep, including an afternoon nap of one to three hours. For a one- to three-year-old, nighttime sleep and daytime naps can:

- Ensure proper growth, as growth hormones are released during sleep.
- Improve your child's mood and behavior.
- Increases your child's attention span.
- Boost your child's learning.
- Reduce the risk of daytime injuries.

---

40 https://www.huffpost.com/entry/8-new-ways-sleep-benefits_b_6437974

- Help your child sleep better in general (naps help you child get better sleep at night).

You might wonder how a sleep routine is a mindfulness activity, but just as meditation gives your mind a break from its incessant thoughts, sleep gives your mind and body the chance to heal, renew, and rest.

To be a mindful parent, you need to be attentive, rested, and calm. For your child to be happy and healthy and able to focus on his critical work of discovery and play, you need to ensure he gets the rest required for optimal growth and development.

FOR YOUR TODDLER...

Here are some basic routines and a sample schedule for your toddler (with a suggested timeframe), as well as some ideas for incorporating mindfulness. (Note: This schedule includes just one nap, but you may need to include an additional morning nap for younger toddlers.)

Create a good morning wake-up plan (7:30–9:00 a.m.).

Just as you need a positive morning routine, so does your toddler—but you need to be the one to provide it for her and determine her morning schedule.

If your child awakens before you finish your own morning routine, it's perfectly fine to let her have a few minutes of quiet time in her crib before you get her out. You can explain to her that "morning crib time" is part of your daily routine, and she will learn to occupy herself for a few minutes until you are ready to begin the day.

Put some books or safe toys in the crib at night for her to find in the morning to keep her occupied. This teaches her to self-soothe and learn to play by herself, a skill that all children need to learn.

As an example, Steve keeps a basket of toys by his oldest son's bed. Typically, his son will get up in the morning, grab a few items, and play in his bed for fifteen minutes as he "starts his day."

Once you get your child out of the crib, your morning routine for her might include:

- Cuddle time with you in the bed or rocking chair.
- Getting dressed and brushing teeth.
- Eating breakfast and cleaning up.
- Watching a morning educational TV program for thirty minutes.
- Getting in the car with a book or toy (if you work or have other children who you need to drive to school).

Plan a play (and chore) activity at home (9:00–9:45 a.m.).

After the early morning routine, you might plan a quiet or creative activity for your child to do by herself, giving you time to clean up, do some laundry, or finish a project.

You may want to use part of this time for your toddler to help you with a simple chore, teaching her that even the youngest family members must contribute.

Toddlers can...

- Pick up toys.

- Fold towels.
- Match socks and sort clothes.
- Put laundry in a basket and deliver clothes.
- Sort utensils and put them away.
- Dust surfaces with a duster.
- Pull up a bed.
- Feed pets.

Once chores are over, set a timer for twenty to thirty minutes (or whatever your child's attention span is) for a play activity, and give yourself a cushion of a few minutes to transition from playtime to the next activity. You may want to plan a couple of activities during this timeframe.

If you have a craft area, your toddler might...

- Paint with watercolors.
- Have fun with play-dough.
- Make a collage.
- Make a thumbprint picture.
- Color in a coloring book.
- Put stickers in a sticker book.

If you don't want to pull out crafts, your toddler can...

- Work on an age-appropriate puzzle.
- Listen to an audio story.
- Play with figurines or toy cars.
- Play with Legos or blocks.
- String beads or sort buttons.

- Play with paper dolls.
- Work on an object-matching game.

Once the timer goes off, tell your toddler it's time to finish up play, and give her another minute or two before you help her clean up or put toys away. Let her know that once you are finished cleaning up, it will be time for a snack—a positive motivation to transition away from playtime.

Plan a healthy snack and talk about mindful eating (9:45–10:00 a.m.).

Being a mindful parent means being attentive to what you feed your child and helping her pay more attention to what she is eating. Use snack time as an opportunity to teach your toddler about the benefits of healthy eating, and what foods are good for you.

When you give your child a snack, talk about how the food is helping her grow, making her bones stronger, and allowing her eyes to see better. Discuss the relationship between food and energy, mood, and being smart.

"Eating this apple and peanut butter will make you feel happy and strong for our outing to the park this afternoon."

Also, show your child how to eat mindfully by noticing and talking about the tastes, smells, and sensations of eating. Food shouldn't be gobbled down without thought or gratitude. It should be savored, appreciated, and enjoyed.

Ask your child to notice three things about what she is eating. Or ask questions to inspire your child to pay more attention to the food.

- Are those carrots soft or crunchy?
- What fruit does the yogurt taste like?
- Close your eyes and tell me what you smell.
- Is that banana salty or sweet?
- How does that cup of cocoa feel in your hands?

Develop a gratitude moment with your child during snack time. Talk to her about where food comes from, how it grows, the people who produce it, and the grocery store workers who put it on the shelves.

Discuss how wonderful it is that these people help bring food to your table so that you can enjoy it during snack time and at other meals. Ask your child about the foods she is most grateful for and why. This is a way to teach your child not to take things for granted—even the essentials like food.

If you need some ideas for healthy snacks for your toddler, you can find hundreds of creative suggestions on Pinterest or by looking at this master list[41] of ideas from the Yummy Toddler Food site.

Join a play group for lunch (10:00 a.m.–12:30 p.m.).

A playdate or play group is important for toddlers as they begin to learn social development, so try to schedule in some kind of social activity (perhaps with a packed lunch) a few times a week.

---

41   https://www.yummytoddlerfood.com/recipes/snacks-recipes/master-snack
-list/

A "mommy/daddy and me" type program is a great way to let young toddlers interact with other children, even if they aren't playing with them or interacting directly.

You can teach your young toddler to greet other children and adults, follow directions, and learn "back and forth" play (the prelude to sharing) by taking turns with your child. "It's Mommy's turn with the toy. Now it's Sarah's turn."

Older toddlers will begin playing side-by-side with other children, but they have a hard time sharing, as their behavior is guided by egocentric thinking. This is the time to model sharing with your little one by showing how you (or another child) are sharing a toy.

An older toddler will want to play with other children, and even though sharing is still hard, she will find ways to compromise in order to maintain cooperative play.

A supervised play group with other parents and children is a good place to help your three-year-old prepare for the later social interactions in preschool and beyond.

These group activities are perfect environments to teach your toddler to notice and understand the feelings of others. If you see another child who is frustrated or sad, help your child identify the emotions.

"Jackson is mad because it's not his turn to ride the scooter."

"Zoe is crying because she's tired and it's nap time."

You can begin to teach your child empathy for her playmates' feelings by comparing the emotional situation to something your child has felt.

"Jackson is angry because it's not his turn on the scooter. You feel mad sometimes when you have to take turns, don't you?"

Share a mindfulness moment before nap time (12:45–2:30 p.m.).

Once your playdate or play group hour is over, the time after lunch but before a nap is a good time to introduce a mindfulness activity to your older toddler.

This quiet time with your child in her room is also a peaceful transition from the activity of the day to a period of sleep and rest.

You can teach your child a mini-meditation or breathing exercise that introduces her to the concept of being present and calm. However, toddlers don't have long attention spans, so you'll need to devise a meditation plan that is fun and short. Here are four ideas to consider:

1. The Bell Game

Using a meditation chime or bell, teach your child to be still and quiet for increasing amounts of time, which will help with focus and self-control and set the stage for learning how to meditate.

- Ask your child to sit in a chair or crossed-legged on the floor with her hands resting in her lap.

- Let her know that when you ring the bell, she should close her eyes and sit without talking, just listening to the fading sound of the bell. When you ring the bell again, she can open her eyes and talk.

- Start with fifteen seconds of quiet time and gradually increase the amount of time your child can sit quietly.

- Get a calendar and some fun stickers, and every time your child successfully sits quietly until the bell rings, she can put a sticker on the calendar. When one week is filled with stickers, offer a reward or treat to reinforce her efforts.

2. Blow the Candle

This mindfulness activity is better for older toddlers (or pre-schoolers) who follow directions, since you'll be using a lit candle. It teaches your child the basics of a simple breathing meditation.

- Have your child sit cross-legged on the floor facing you. Show him how to place his hands face-up on each knee or in his lap.
- Ask your child to take three deep breaths. You'll need to show him how to do this.
- Put a candle in a holder and light it. Instruct your child not to touch the candle but to keep his hands on his crossed knees.
- Then tell him to gently blow out of his mouth very slowly toward the flame—but without blowing out the flame. It takes focus and concentration to blow softly without blowing it out, so you will need to demonstrate.
- Have him go slowly and pause between breaths. Try to get him to blow three to five times without extinguishing the flame.
- Use the same sticker and reward system mentioned for the Bell Game.

3. Watch the Flame

This mindfulness activity combines elements of the previous two, helping your child focus on a lit candle for extended periods between bell rings.

- Ask your child to sit in a chair or crossed-legged on the floor with her hands resting in her lap.

- Light the candle, ring the bell, and let her know that she should stare at the flame without looking at anything else until you ring the bell again. Staring at a flame creates a trance-like affect that toddlers (and all of us) find mesmerizing.

- Begin with ten to fifteen seconds, and gradually increase the amount of time between bell rings.

- Use the same sticker and reward system mentioned above.

4. Mantra and Breathing Ritual

Devise a short, simple, and positive mantra for your toddler to teach him to use positive affirmations. You will combine saying this mantra with a simple breathing practice. Try using three or four "I am" statements for the mantra, like, "I am happy. I am healthy. I am loved."

- Create a meditation space for your child with a rug or towel on the floor and soft music playing. Build anticipation for your child as you set up your "mindfulness moment."

- Ask your child to sit cross-legged on the floor with his hands resting on his legs or facing up on his knees.

- Repeat the mantra to your child and say it together a few times so he can repeat it easily.

- Breathe in together, and on the out-breath, speak the first part of the mantra: "I am happy." (You may need to show him how the first time.)

- Take another inhalation, and on the out-breath, say the next part of the mantra: "I am healthy."

- Follow the same instructions for the final part of the mantra: "I am loved."

- Repeat the breathing and mantra series two or three times, or as many as your toddler has patience for.

You may need to experiment with these activities to see which one works best for your child. Or you might want to mix them up if your child grows bored with the practice. All of these activities can be used for preschoolers as well as toddlers.

After you finish your mindful moment, it will be time for your toddler's nap. Be sure there are at least three hours between the end of your child's nap and bedtime. You should avoid letting your sleepyhead nap past 4:00 p.m. or he'll have problems falling asleep at bedtime.

Create a post-nap transition (2:30–3:00 p.m.).

Your toddler will likely feel groggy and needy of your attention after a nap, and require a transition between sleep and activity. If possible, allow some time after his nap to gently awaken without feeling rushed or forced into interaction or play.

This quiet time also gives you a few meditative or gratitude moments for just sitting and being still—something that's hard to do with a toddler in the house.

As quickly as your toddler is growing and seeing himself as a separate person from you, this quiet transition time can help maintain your close physical bond.

You may want to...

- Cuddle in the rocking chair for a few minutes.
- Offer some milk or a small snack while he sits in your lap.
- Put on an audiobook so he can listen quietly while waking up.
- Sing a song to him as you rub his back.
- Let him sit near you with a comfort item (pacifier or blanket) while you meditate or do a chore.
- Carry him outside to look at nature or watch the rain for a few minutes.
- Sit quietly with the family pet.

Not all toddlers require this transition time after a nap. Some wake up ready to take on the world and begin the next adventure. But if your child needs some calm time in between sleep and activity, use this time to his (and your) advantage as a mindfulness respite.

Develop an outdoor play habit (3:00–4:30 p.m.).

It's sad to acknowledge that children in the U.S. are more sedentary than ever, spending more than 80% of their time sitting indoors. In fact, today's kids spend half the time that their parents spent outside as children.

The lack of outside play is connected to increased obesity rates, attention and focus problems, and lifelong health problems. It also stunts a child's appreciation for and connection to nature, an elemental mindfulness practice that should be part of their lives forever.

Being outside can bring a sense of calm to you and your child, reducing stress and cultivating a connection with the earth and all of the sights, sounds, smells, and emotions that the natural world provides.

Making outdoor activity a part of your daily routine, even in inclement weather, is an invaluable gift to your child—and there's no more receptive participant than a toddler.

Toddlers learn through play and are naturally curious, active explorers. Being outside gives them the freedom they crave, allowing them to move, touch, run, and jump. The various surfaces, slopes, and heights available outdoors provide a one-of-a-kind learning lab for little ones to develop balance and coordination.

You've probably noticed that, once your child is outside, she is almost instantly happy to go run and play. If you commit to making outdoor play part of your daily routine, it will become a positive habit that will serve your child as she grows. For children and adults, nothing can replace the mindfulness benefits of an appreciation for the natural world.

Open, unstructured outdoor play in which your toddler can explore and move around freely with few rules (except for safety rules) is exhilarating for her. She can be fully present with every experience of her choosing, without a battle of wills over what she can and can't do.

If you want to enhance the mindfulness aspect of outdoor play for your child, a little creative forethought provides additional options for your child's experience of nature. Here are four ideas to consider:

1. Explore your senses.

As you head to a nearby park, or just to your backyard, walk with your child and ask her:

- What do you see?
- What do you hear?
- What do you feel?
- What do you smell?

Encourage her to notice the various details of the natural world and put them into words.

- Pick up an acorn or a piece of moss and talk about the different textures.
- Ask your toddler to find a bug and watch it together for a few minutes.
- Feel the prickly evergreen needles on a pine tree.
- Bend down with your toddler to smell a flower or blow dandelion seeds and watch them fly away.
- Point out the sounds of birds calling or the wind blowing.
- If it's raining or snowing outside, ask your toddler to open her mouth to taste the cold raindrop or freezing snowflake.

A little guidance and direction from you can open your toddler's eyes to the subtleties of nature that she might not notice.

2. Become a tree.

Point out to your child how trees are tall, strong, and have deep roots that hold them in the ground and connect them to the earth. Talk about how trees make us feel calm and happy, how they create oxygen (or air) that helps us breath. They grow to be the oldest living species on earth, offer habitation and food for wildlife, produce fruits and nuts that we eat, and provide the wood we use for fuel, furniture, tools, and other products.

Now ask your toddler to become like a tree (or do this together). Take off his shoes (weather permitting) so his toes can dig into the ground and become deep roots. Ask him to stand straight and tall so his body can be the strong and steadfast trunk of the tree.

Then he can spread his arms and fingers to be the branches and twigs where birds and other animals live. He can even wave his arms when the wind blows and wiggle his fingers like rustling leaves.

Remind your child to take a deep breath and blow out, just as a tree shares oxygen with the world around it. Finish this activity by hugging a tree (yes, become tree huggers) and thanking the tree for all it does to support and protect us.

3. Stack some rocks.

We've been stacking rocks since the dawn of time—or at least the dawn of mankind. Stone stacks (called cairns) have prehistoric origins, marking burial grounds and shrines around the world.

You may have seen modern versions of these stacked stones in miniature form, little Zen-like expressions of calm and peace randomly created by people enjoying the natural world.

Creating these small stone stacks requires concentration, slow movement, and patience—abilities that typically elude a toddler.

But you can quickly harness her interest and attention if you show her how to build one.

Searching for stones of various sizes and stacking them in a tower is a toddler's idea of an important job to tackle, and she'll do it with fervor and focus. And if you live near a creek or dry riverbed, you and your child will have plenty to work with for a fun mindfulness outdoor activity.

For small children, rock stacking is more challenging than stacking blocks since rocks are irregularly shaped. But with practice, your child will figure out the physics of balancing different-sized rocks on top of each other—and the irrepressible joy of knocking them all down again.

Speaking of knocking them down, the stone-stacking practice has become a bit controversial, as some naturalists consider it destructive given how pervasive it's become in national and state parks. Consider dismantling your rock stacks if your busy little juggernaut hasn't destroyed them first.

4. Watch the clouds.

At some point during your playtime outdoors, your toddler will start to wind down or get bored. When you notice a yawn or some fussiness, redirect your child and spread out a blanket to enjoy some cloud gazing.

Small children are often surprised to discover that clouds are always moving. They look like fluffy permanent structures in the sky until you pay close attention and see them slowly and gently floating along.

Ask your little one to lie down on his back and look at the clouds. Wait a few minutes to see if he notices the movement. If not, point it out and talk about how the wind makes clouds move just like it makes the leaves blow on trees. Then point out different shapes you see in the clouds and ask your toddler what he sees. A lion? A dragon? A funny face?

There are so many possible options for mindfulness activities for your child when you have a regular outdoor routine. Don't let rain or cold weather deter you. Bundle up and use the weather as an opportunity for awareness and joy. In addition to the activities outlined here, you and your toddler can...

- Carry a basket to gather nature items for a later art project.
- Create a magic "nature spot" in your yard for your toddler to enjoy.
- Carry a shovel and pail for digging and making mud pies.
- Take a "rain walk" to splash in puddles and feel raindrops.
- Walk barefoot in the grass.
- Gather nature items and tell a story using the items.
- Roll down a hill.
- Have a scavenger hunt so your toddler can find items in nature.
- Blow bubbles outside and watch the wind carry them away.

Set up a pre-dinner activity (4:30–5:30 p.m.).

The hour or so before dinner can be particularly difficult for parents. You're trying to prepare the meal while keeping an eye on an active toddler.

Toddlers, especially those who are down to one nap, can be cranky or unusually hyperactive in the late afternoon. And parents feel exhausted in the late afternoon after a full day of working, doing chores, and/or taking care of toddlers.

As a result, your first instinct might be to turn on the TV so you can have some uninterrupted time to prepare dinner. Television is fine in moderation, but as a mindful parent, you'll want other options so your toddler doesn't spend too much time watching TV.

The American Academy of Pediatrics (AAP) recommends that children younger than eighteen months have no screen time at all, so there's that. Kids ages two to five should spend no more than an hour a day in front of screens of any kind–TV, tablet, phone, or computer. (You'll read more about electronics and digital devices in the preschooler section.)

You can make thoughtful decisions about how this pre-dinner time should play out by paying attention to your child's physical and emotional state in the late afternoon.

Does he tend to have plenty of energy and seem overactive and excitable? Or is your child fussy, tired, or needy?

Use your child's behavior as a guide for directing his time in the best way.

For the active, energetic toddler, you want to harness some of that energy so he winds down before bedtime. But it may not be realistic to insist he sit quietly looking at books.

Here are four alternative ideas to work off late-afternoon energy:

1. Walk on Pillows Game

Along with your toddler, gather all of the sofa and chair cushions and pillows you can find and line them up in a row on the floor (staying away from hard obstacles in case of falls).

Ask your toddler to walk back and forth from one end of the pillows to the other without falling off. This is tougher than it appears for a toddler who is still trying to strengthen gross motor skills. It takes focus, balance, and coordination.

Challenge her to do the "pillow walk" as many times as possible, praising her for her efforts to keep her interested in the game.

Once she is done with the game, ask her to return all of the pillows where they belong, which is a fun activity itself that requires matching, memory, and physical effort.

2. Balloon Badminton

Tape a paint stir stick or popsicle stick to a sturdy paper plate to create a badminton racket. Then blow up a balloon or two (in case one pops). Give both items to your toddler and instruct him to keep the balloon off the ground using the "badminton" racket.

Be sure you clear plenty of space so your child won't bump into furniture, as he'll have his eyes in the air. Set a timer for thirty seconds, then a minute, and even longer as he gains more control and coordination keeping the balloon in the air.

If you have other children, you can make two rackets for back-and-forth play. Just be sure an older child doesn't try to "beat" the younger one in a competitive game or you'll spend more time being a referee than preparing dinner.

3. Move Like an Animal

Print drawings or images of a variety of animals and put the images facedown in a stack. Ask your toddler to choose an image and then become that animal, going from room to room acting out the part.

Your toddler can become...

- A bird
- A cat
- An elephant
- An alligator
- A snake
- A bear
- A frog
- A penguin
- A kangaroo
- A lion
- A monkey
- A dinosaur
- A turkey

This may require some supervision from you depending on the excitability of your child, but you can instruct him to become a "sleepy baby" version of the animal to calm him down.

Acting out various animals is a fun way for your little one to use new muscles, work off some energy, and use his imagination.

If your toddler is tired and cranky and has no energy for the games mentioned above, have some ideas in mind to keep him engaged so that he doesn't beg to zone out in front of the TV. Any of the quiet morning activities we mentioned earlier will do the trick. However, if you want to make this time something your toddler looks forward to, you can create daily "Quiet Boxes."

4. Quiet Box Time

Assemble daily "Quiet Boxes" that you offer your child every afternoon during the time you prepare dinner. Purchase seven inexpensive plastic boxes (a 16-quart tub with lid is a good size) and label them with the days of the week.

On Sundays, fill each box with a variety of quiet activities for your toddler, changing out the activities each week. You don't have to purchase new items for the Quiet Boxes. Fill them with games and activities that you already have but that your toddler may not have seen in a while. Some ideas include:

- Coloring pages and crayons
- Sticker books
- Simple puzzles
- Figurines and toy cars
- Shells and stones
- Beads for stringing
- Picture books
- Magnets
- Cards with pictures
- Stacking toys
- Sorting games

- Peg board

It's fine if you repeat some of these activities during the week. Just have enough of a mix that your child sees each box as something new and fun.

Plan a simple dinner ritual. (5:30–6:30 p.m.).

Creating the dinner ritual we outlined earlier can be challenging with a small child. As much as we'd like dinner to be a calm and peaceful affair where everyone sits together amicably, things are unpredictable with a two- to three-year-old.

One parenting writer complained on her blog[42] that she finds "dinner time with my toddler to be just about as enjoyable as getting my teeth scraped at the dentist."

Food gets summarily rejected ("This is yucky!") or even hurled across the room in protest. Getting your toddler to eat what you serve can become a battle of the wills, and more often than not, you lose—especially if dessert or some other bribe is a negotiating tactic.

Toddlers generally need to eat earlier than adults so they can go to bed early. It isn't always possible for a busy family to sit down together at 5:30 or 6:00 for a meal, but if you can make it happen, it's an excellent practice to develop in your family to foster connection and a certain amount of ceremony that's lacking in modern life.

Our advice for mindful parents is to keep the dinner hour as simple, enjoyable, and stress-free as possible, for both you and your child.

---

42   https://www.kveller.com/article/dinnertime-with-toddlers/

Here are four rituals that we suggest:

1. Bring your toddler to the table.

A family dinner means that everyone is at the table, even your toddler—as long as he can maintain a semblance of decorum (no food throwing, tantrums, playing with food, etc.).

Toddlers want to feel they are "big boys or girls" and that they can sit at the grown-ups table rather than being relegated to the high chair in the kitchen.

The family dinner is the perfect opportunity to help your little one learn social skills, manners, and gratitude. Discuss your expectations or the "dinner table rules" before you sit down. Develop your own rituals (setting the table, music, candles, etc.) that make this family time unique and special.

2. Let your toddler decide.

We're not suggesting that you let her choose ice cream for dinner every night. The idea is to put several nutritious food options on her plate that you know she likes that create a balanced meal.

Don't make a big deal about whether or not she eats what you present. Food is for nutrition and health, so you don't need to praise for eating or shame for rejecting.

Your child won't starve or get scurvy if she doesn't eat her vegetables daily, and she will eventually appreciate healthy eating if that's one of your family values.

Make portions small so you don't waste food, and if she only eats one item and rejects the rest, be okay with that. Wrap it up, and, if she's hungry later, you can offer the food she left on her plate.

Prioritize healthy foods first by ensuring your toddler eats her meal before you offer any sweets or other nutritionally deficient foods.

Also, consider avoiding a regular dessert after dinner. You don't want to train your toddler to fight with you about eating the meal just to get the dessert. Offer sweets sparingly and randomly, with no strings attached.

3. Keep offering new foods.

You'll discover quickly what foods your toddler does and doesn't like. But you should still continue to offer new foods or bites of your adult dinner to help expand your child's palette.

Don't make a big deal of it if the offer is rejected. Don't go on and on about how delicious it is or zoom a bite to her mouth on your airplane fork. "Mmm mmm, these liver tips and onions are divine. Have a bite!"

This will only reveal how invested you are in what she is eating, and she'll discover your Achilles heel and use it to her tiny, mischievous advantage. Just say, "Okay," if your offer is rejected and move on.

4. Keep meals simple.

If you spend hours whipping up a chicken Florentine and your toddler does his impression of gagging, you're bound to be aggravated after investing so much time preparing the meal.

Foods with multiple ingredients mixed together like casseroles, stews, stir-fries, and curries often get a thumbs down from toddlers.

Create "real" meals for the adults (and older kids) in the house, but keep dinners simple and recognizable for your toddler.

Pasta with jarred sauce, English muffin pizza, chopped fruit, cubed chicken, mashed sweet potato, and veggies with dips are simple (and generally) acceptable choices for toddlers.

You can disguise the dreaded vegetables in pasta sauce (puree the sauce with zucchini or spinach), in muffins like zucchini or carrot muffins, or in smoothies.

Create a bath and bedtime ritual (6:30–7:30 p.m.).

This is the most gratifying part of the day for most parents—not only because it is so sweet and special with your little one, but also because, once completed, you get some blessed time to yourself (yay!).

The long march between 4:00 p.m. and bedtime can feel eternal, especially if you've been up and at it since 6:00 a.m. All you want is a warm bath, a good book, and a glass of wine.

But first...you need to wind down the day for your toddler without just going through the motions to get to that glass of wine. Take a deep breath and remind yourself how tender and enjoyable this before-bed time can be and how important it is for your child.

"Environmental rituals generally change the ambience of the home to give the child conscious or unconscious cues that sleep time is coming," says Dr. Harvey Karp for Fatherly.[43]

---

43 https://www.fatherly.com/parenting/bedtime-routines-bedtime-rituals-sleep-young-children/

If you love a warm bath in a spa-like atmosphere, create this for your toddler too—an experience that will calm and relax him in preparation for sleep.

Bath time "is the ideal transition from day to night, activity to sleep; it teaches self-care, the importance of winding down, and is just a great moment for easy parent/child conversation," say the writers at Gwyneth Paltrow's blog, Goop.[44]

Before you begin the bath, your toddler may need to use the potty (if potty-trained), and you will want to brush his teeth. Get these things out of the way before he gets in the bath so you can maintain the soothing transition from tub to bed.

Keep the environment peaceful and free from stimulating distractions so bath time doesn't become a raucous episode of *Flipper*. Light a few candles (out of reach), put on some soft music, and keep bath toys to a minimum. Avoid filling the tub with squirt guns, loud squeakers, and any toy that inspires your toddler to hurl it out of the tub.

Use this time to connect physically with your child, gently washing him head to toe, paying close attention to folds and crevices. Wash his hair last (so your toddler isn't sitting in a tub of shampoo suds, which can be irritating) while giving him a relaxing head rub.

For your own mindful moment, take time to appreciate the softness of your toddler's skin, his sweet smell after you wash him, and the beautiful way he looks in candlelight. Savor this special moment with all of your heart, as you won't be bathing your children forever.

---

44   https://goop.com/wellness/mindfulness/bath-time-rituals-to-put-kids-to -bed/

Try to keep tub time to ten to fifteen minutes so you don't dry out his skin, and so the water doesn't get too cold. Have a soft, fluffy towel ready and wrap him up in it once you remove your little tadpole from the tub. Finish bath time with a full-body, fragrance-free-moisturizer massage, a clean diaper or Pull-Up, and some soft, warm pajamas (that your toddler helped choose).

Immediately after a bath, Barrie would take her children to the nursery to read a story or two, sing a favorite before-bed song, and rock for a few minutes before putting them into the crib with a hug and kiss.

Every night Barrie would repeat a phrase to her children that her mother said to her before bed: "You're a perfect child of God. God loves you and I love you too." This was a special, memorable part of her evening ritual with her children.

There are other toddler bedtime rituals that might be part of your time with your little one, including:

- Turning the lights down.
- Saying goodnight to the other parent and/or siblings.
- Picking out a book together.
- Breastfeeding (if you are still nursing your child).
- Talking quietly together.
- Deep breathing.
- An affirmation or prayer that you repeat together.
- A gratitude moment.
- A lullaby.
- Cuddle time.
- Closing the curtains or blinds.

- Offering a blanket, favorite stuffed animal, or pacifier.
- Turning on white noise.

All of the routines throughout the day give your toddler a sense of control and security, knowing he can count on you to usher him through the day in a predictable way.

The very nature of being a toddler and growing up requires constant change—learning new skills, adjusting to bodily changes, and letting go of old comforts. Daily routines make these unpredictable changes less daunting when they occur in the context of familiar routines.

You won't be able to stick to your routines every day. You will have other obligations or situations arise that interrupt your schedule. But if your child has the safety of predictable routines most of the time, he will feel less anxious and more able to cope when disruptions do occur.

Forethought, preparation, redirection, empathy, consistency, patience, and routine—these are the essential tools for mindfully parenting a toddler and actually enjoying it. Yes, your little one will test your resolve to remain calm and intentional in your reactions.

You may find the adherence to all of the necessary routines restrictive and boring. You may long for the days when you had an infant that slept more and wasn't as demanding, emotional, and active.

But once you graduate from parenting a toddler, you'll be prepared for just about anything that parenthood can throw at you. You'll have learned mindfulness habits to improve your own life and relationships, as well as the skills to be a more intentional, thoughtful, and value-driven parent.

Your efforts will pay off in the long-term ability to be more creative rather than reactive in your role as a parent, a skill that will continue to serve you in the next phase of parenting your preschooler.

PRESCHOOLERS (AGES 3-5)

Ah, preschoolers—those little bundles of joyful exuberance and budding independence. Your child is not a baby anymore, and though there may be some toddler holdovers (tantrums, defiance, and need for routine), he is learning many new skills and stretching his cognitive abilities.

Your preschooler's maturing physical abilities may make you more confident that his safety isn't as precarious as it was for your toddler. But his curiosity and independence can get him into trouble—he's quick to run off on his own or hop on a scooter without a helmet.

Where your toddler's rebellions were mostly reactionary, your preschooler gleefully engages in willful defiance, looking you right in the eye as he does the thing you just told him not to do. Of course he knows not to pull the dog's tail, but he does it anyway because he wants to test the limits. He now has a more secure identity and uses defiance to assert himself.

At the same time, your preschooler craves limits and needs you to spell them out clearly despite wanting to show off his newfound autonomy.

Your job as a mindful parent is to help your preschooler find solutions to the underlying problems that often trigger some defiant behavior (like your child continuing to disrupt his brother's game because he feels left out). And of course you'll need to practice patience and consistency just as you did when your child was a toddler.

Although your child is no longer a toddler, his burgeoning skills and sense of independence may fool you into thinking he is more cognitively advanced than he is. But all of his bravado can be misleading. A younger preschooler isn't able to understand a request or instruction from you that involves thinking, vocabulary, or listening skills he hasn't yet developed.

As you did when parenting your toddler, you need to educate yourself on your preschooler's developmental stages and what you can realistically expect from your child. Punishing or admonishing a child for not following rules or meeting expectations beyond his abilities is a sure formula for creating an anxious and insecure child—or maybe a more defiant one.

It's also helpful to remember that this age group is blissfully egocentric. Preschoolers believe that everything in the world revolves around them, and they have a hard time understanding another person's viewpoint.

Even so, preschoolers do have strong emotions and can feel compassion for you or friends who show obvious signs of distress. But like toddlers, preschoolers still haven't fully identified what feelings are, so they look to you to help them identify their own feelings and begin to understand the feelings of others.

Despite being self-centered, preschoolers are significantly influenced by important adults, especially parents and teachers. Teaching empathy, social skills, and emotional control should be part of your daily efforts with your preschooler, even if you don't see the results right away. Little minds are soaking up these skills, especially if they are presented in a kind and patient way.

Mindful parenting for your preschooler requires learning how to talk to your child so he will listen and understand—and how to *actively* listen to your child so you can be more discerning in your reactions and instructions.

Discipline for your preschooler isn't about controlling him (he will surely resist); it's about teaching your child how to *control himself* in preparation for the future demands of school and life.

Speaking of school, children in the age range of three to five may be called "preschoolers," but your child may or may not be enrolled in a preschool program. Whether or not your child attends a pre-kindergarten program is a decision you'll need to make consciously, with a clear understanding of your own motivations, the benefits of preschool, and your child's needs.

As we discuss in the mindful parenting strategies for this age group, preschool isn't a necessity but can have many positive benefits for your child, his socialization, and his readiness for kindergarten.

These will be the last few years when you'll have your child with you for most of the day, if you or your spouse stays at home. But whether or not you work outside of the home, the preschool years are the last when you'll be the primary teacher and (as your child grows older) main influence on your child.

Many parents see these few years when their preschooler is learning at a such a rapid rate and soaking up so much information as a pivotal time for teaching their children the skills, values, and self-regulation so necessary for future success and happiness.

You may not be as physically active with your preschooler as you were when chasing a toddler, but you will be more mentally and emotionally taxed as you guide your child toward readiness for school and life. And you will still need to draw on mindfulness to help you maintain your energy and equanimity during these special years.

It's normal to grow impatient when your preschooler insists on doing everything himself, asks you a thousand and one questions a day, and wants to pull out every craft project in the closet. That's why continuing a meditation practice and maintaining other personal mindfulness practices is an ongoing necessity for your self-care.

And preschool children are ripe for learning and participating in mindfulness activities themselves, as their attention spans are now a bit longer. The activities mentioned in the toddler section will still work well for your older child, but we outline some additional practices in this section that you can share with your preschooler.

What to Expect during This Stage

Your child has the fine motor skills to dress herself and the gross motor skills to ride a tricycle. She is coloring, drawing, cutting, and pasting her way through piles of art supplies to explore and develop her creative potential. She's ready to learn her numbers and letters and to make simple decisions.

Most parents wish they could bottle their kids' energy at this age, since they never seem to run out of it and are buzzing with energy when not expending it. They love to play and explore, as this is how they learn and adapt to their environment.

Your child's favorite questions right now are probably "Why?" and "How?" But remember when you answer that preschoolers think very concretely and literally, and to a preschool child, things are as they appear to be. (Abstract and figurative thinking don't happen until early adolescence.)

Your child is getting better at using the potty and may or may not wake up dry. She's also more likely to share her toys (sometimes) and listen more to others.

Your preschooler is also becoming a more cooperative player despite her rascally defiance on occasion. What she learns from your conversations and from the books you read to her helps her develop social skills.

She wants to understand more and to find solutions to her own problems, and she might not tell you what she's up to if she's intent on learning something new. Don't be surprised if she walks into the house caked in mud or carrying something alive and squirming; most people only wish they felt as connected to nature as their preschoolers do.

What Your Preschooler Needs during This Stage

Your preschooler wants to learn about everything in his world and to understand words and numbers. He needs for you to spend time playing with him, singing and reading to him, and praising him for his accomplishments. He'll want more space to explore and to try new things, and he'll test the limits of your parental authority as well as your patience.

He needs to understand your expectations of him and to know you'll be there for him when he needs you. He needs to be given choices and to be trusted with the opportunity to learn things his own way.

In fact, your preschooler wants more opportunities to learn how to do things for himself. Most of all, he needs to be reminded of your unconditional love for him, and to know he's worth your time and undivided attention.

Listen to your child tell you about what he's learned, what he's excited about, what's bothering him, and what he'd love to do when he gets the chance. Give him opportunities to meet and interact with new people, to demonstrate what he's learned, to create new things, and to indulge his curiosity.

You can still apply many of the mindful parenting and mindfulness skills covered in the infant and toddler sections to your preschooler. If, for example, you experience more of the "terrible threes" than the "terrible twos," the sections on tantrums and mindful discipline will certainly apply to your older child.

And like toddlers, preschoolers need routine and structure—although your routines may be different now, especially if your child is in preschool or day care. The toddler sections on establishing routines and rituals will equally benefit your preschool-aged child.

Your main role as preschooler parents is to encourage and celebrate your child's growing sense of self while gently guiding him with positive reinforcement, limits, and boundaries. Try to stay as present as possible with your child, recognizing the brief window of time you have before he hops on the school bus and begins a life that is increasingly more independent and separated from you. Enjoy these special few years together with your little one, even as you work to prepare him for his life ahead.

Now that you know the basics of your preschooler's development and needs, let's move on to the specific mindful parenting skills for this stage.

19. Help Your Preschooler Identify Feelings

When your child was a toddler, you helped her name her feelings and began to point out the feelings of others as a precursor to developing empathy. But toddlers still have a ways to go before they can talk about their feelings rather than impulsively acting on them.

By the preschool ages, however, your child has a slightly more sophisticated grasp of feelings but still has difficulty verbalizing them without first acting them out. Now is the time to use mindful parenting to help your child develop more emotional awareness. With your guidance, your preschooler can:

- Begin to understand why she gets angry, sad, upset, etc.
- Learn to recognize how intense emotions begin.
- Develop skills to cope with anger and manage it.

You can help your child become more emotionally intelligent by taking the time to teach her the skills of feeling identification and emotional self-control—skills that will serve her well in all of her relationships for the rest of her life.

That may sound like a tall order for parents who don't have a PhD in child psychology, but teaching these skills isn't difficult if you are motivated to guide your child and have some tools in your parenting toolbox. Maintaining your cool during your preschooler's emotional outbursts may prove to be harder—but remember, you mastered that during the terrible twos! You know how to breathe through these difficult moments so you can be present enough to help your child through them.

Here are some skills you can teach your child (and even apply to yourself) when she is experiencing and acting on intense emotions.

Draw Emotions

When your child is experiencing intense emotions of anger, frustration, or sadness, pull out paper and crayons and ask her to draw how she is feeling (as soon as she is calm enough to draw).

She may not be able to verbalize what's going on in her mind and body, but she can use form and color to symbolize the swirl of feelings inside of her. Talk with her about what she's drawing and help her put words to her artistic expressions.

You can even draw feelings yourself and talk about your drawings with your child: "These red and black scribbles show my angry feelings." "This blue face in the corner of the page shows me feeling sad."

Ask "It Seems Like" Questions

You can help your preschooler learn to verbalize his feelings by asking him some simple questions to help him identify his emotions. To do this, you must be in tune with your child's feelings by noticing his behavior, expressions, and body language.

Anger is easy to identify, but frustration, embarrassment, and sadness require you to really pay attention and recognize more subtle signs.

Once you have a good idea of what your child is feeling, ask questions like:

- "It seems like you are angry and hurt that your brother won't play with you."
- "It seems like you are sad that the baby dinosaur lost his mama."
- "It seems like you are frustrated that you can't tie your shoe right now."

Acknowledging your child's feelings makes him feel validated and understood. Hopefully, your child will confirm the feelings that you've acknowledged, and you can discuss how to put these feelings into words the next time.

"The next time you feel angry, use your words to say how you feel rather than hitting your brother. Hitting people isn't allowed."

"When you feel frustrated that you can't do something, tell me about it rather than throwing your shoe. You could hurt someone by throwing things."

Identify Physical Reactions

When we feel angry, sad, frustrated, or hurt, we often feel our emotions physically in our bodies. We clench our teeth, feel pressure behind our eyes, have knots in our stomachs, or feel hot and shaky.

Help your child become more mindful of the physicality of emotions by asking her to point out where in her body she is feeling her anger or frustration.

Often these physical reactions occur before emotions begin to spill out in negative behavior. Talk to your child about paying attention to these warning signs before an emotional outburst, and give her options for calming down once she notices these signs.

She might...

- Practice deep breathing.
- Count to ten over and over until she calms down.
- Draw her feelings on paper.
- Punch a pillow or punching bag, or do something else physical to release energy.

When one of Barrie's daughters was a preschooler, she would go to her room, close the door, and sing about her frustrations or anger, making up her own songs about how she was feeling.

These are excellent coping skills for all of us—not just preschoolers.

Role-Play

Identify some of the most common triggering situations that upset your child and cause emotional outbursts or meltdowns. Then, during a calm period, play a role-play game to help your child prepare for these emotional storms.

You can start by saying something like, "Remember the other day how mad you were when Daddy wouldn't let you climb on that tall jungle gym? Let's act out a story about how you can use your words instead of yelling."

Make the game fun and light so there's some laughter mixed in with the lesson. When the critical moment comes and your child acts out using words and emotional self-control, offer a lot of praise and reinforcement.

Talk with your child about possible future situations in which he can use the skills he has just practiced.

Role Model

Your child isn't the only one who has storms of emotions that roll through during the day. You are likely to feel a variety of negative emotions that your child, with her sensitivity to your moods and body language, is sure to pick up on.

Rather than taking out your frustrations on your child or in front of her—or trying to pretend that you are feeling fine when you aren't—use your words with your child to model the very behavior you want to see in her. "I am feeling sad right now because my friend hurt my feelings."

If the source of your negative feelings is your child's actions, be sure to use "I" statements about the behavior rather than about the child herself. "I feel angry right now because you didn't put away the toys like I asked. I'm going to take a time-out to calm down, and then we can talk about it."

Your child is always watching you and learning from your behavior. Practice using your words and "I" statements not only with your child, but also with your spouse or partner. If you and your spouse express your anger or frustrations by yelling, criticizing, or hurling passive aggressive comments, you are teaching your child to do the same.

Check Internal "Weather"

In her book, *Sitting Still Like a Frog*,[45] author Eline Snel invites children to "summon the weather report that best describes [their] feelings at the moment."

Ask your child if he is feeling bright and sunny or cloudy and rainy?

Is a storm brewing, or is the weather calm?

You can even look at pictures of different weather scenarios to help your child identify his interior barometer. As you talk about his internal weather, discuss the way emotions change just as the weather does. Feelings come and go, but they don't define us.

This mindfulness activity shows your child how to observe their current emotional state without overly attaching to the emotions. When we pay attention to our internal weather, what we see can help us anticipate the need for self-control or self-compassion.

As Eline Snel describes it, your child can understand, "I am not the downpour, but I notice that it is raining; I am not a scaredy-cat, but I realize that sometimes I have this big scared feeling somewhere near my throat."

Be the Pond

Another way to teach your preschooler to mindfully observe emotions without attaching to them or judging them is by telling a story of a pond and the fish that swim in the pond.

---

45   https://www.amazon.com/Sitting-Still-Like-Frog-Mindfulness-ebook/dp/B00GS6H3E6

Ask your child to close her eyes and describe all of the fish in the pond. She will see a happy fish, a sad fish, an angry fish, a frustrated fish, etc. Your child's job is to *be the pond* who is noticing all the fish. The pond doesn't care which fish are swimming, but rather just observes the fish as they swim by.

You can remind your preschooler to "be the pond" any time she has strong emotions like anger. Remind her that she isn't the angry fish—she's the pond noticing the fish. In other words, let your child know that she isn't her emotions of anger or sadness. These are just feelings (or fish).

Let your child know that the pond is so much more than all of the fish that swim within it. The pond is calm and wise and knows that fish of all types (all emotions) come and go, but they can't change the pond.

Understanding Physical Causes

When we are tired, hungry, or ill, none of us are at our best. It's much more difficult to control our emotions and be on our best behavior. This is particularly true for children who may not recognize the effects these physical conditions have on their internal worlds.

Talk to your preschooler about the way lack of sleep, hunger, and sickness can make you feel emotionally. When your child is cranky or has a meltdown, ask yourself first whether or not one of these issues could be the culprit.

If so, remind your child about the situation and how it is making them feel. "Remember last night, when you woke up with a bad dream? You didn't get enough sleep last night, and today your tiredness is making you cry."

This recognition will help you manage your expectations and frustrations with your child, as well as help your child see the connection between our bodies and emotions. Understanding this cause and effect allows your child to feel less out of control and confused about powerful emotions.

20. Practice Active Listening and Mindful Communication

Your child looks to you to help him sort through his feelings and provide some comfort when those feelings are overwhelming. An essential part of teaching your child to identify and verbalize his emotions is your ability to practice active or empathic listening with him.

This type of listening is an essential skill in all relationships for children and adults, particularly with the people you're closest to. In this passage from our book *Mindful Relationship Habits*,[46] you can substitute "your child" for "your partner" and the concepts still apply:

> Active and empathic listening has tremendous therapeutic value in your relationship. It allows your partner a safe space to express his or her thoughts and feelings.

> As your partner hears himself talk, he gains more clarity about his feelings or the problem at hand, and becomes better equipped to find a resolution on his or her own or to work on one with you.

> When your partner feels heard, an emotional burden is lifted, and he or she feels less stressed and confused. As the listener, you don't have to agree with everything your partner says. You are listening to learn and to allow your partner to share and vocalize without judgment or anger.

---

46   https://www.amazon.com/Mindful-Relationship-Habits-Practices-Conne ction-ebook/dp/B078HYGSRJ

Active listening with your preschooler involves stopping what you are doing, looking directly at your child, hearing what he has to say with full attention, and then reflecting back to him what you understand about the situation and the way he is feeling about it.

These actions not only allow your child to feel heard and validated but also give him a forum for working through his emotions in an appropriate and healthy way. You don't have to agree with everything he says ("Billy is a bad boy and not my friend anymore!"), but you can reflect back how strong his feelings are about the situation ("You feel so angry at Billy right now.").

Let's say your child comes to you after an incident on the playground with another child who isn't sharing. Here's an example of how you might use active listening:

Your child: "Charlotte won't share her shovel in the sandbox. She's being selfish, and I want to throw sand at her."

You: "It sounds like you're really mad that Charlotte isn't sharing her shovel. Is that right?"

Your child: "Yeah, I'm really, really mad at Charlotte, and I could throw the sand right at her."

You: "You must feel very angry if you could throw sand. But I'm glad you are telling me and using your words instead."

Your child: "I'm not playing with Charlotte anymore. I'm going on the slide now. Watch me climb to the top!"

Your child has communicated how angry she is (so angry she wants to throw sand), and you've validated her feelings while praising her for using words instead of harmful actions. She has diffused her anger because you have listened, and now she can redirect herself to something else.

No matter how invested you may be in a particular outcome, your child needs you to give her the safe space to express her feelings without you interrupting to tell her how to fix the problem, what she may have done wrong, or why she shouldn't feel the way she's feeling.

At some point, you may need to guide her to an apology for her actions, or to a different activity, but in the heat of her intense emotions, she needs to express her feelings and know that she is heard. Eventually, she'll learn how to do that without your presence, perhaps remembering your responses and using them to manage herself.

To summarize the skill of active listening, remember the following steps:

- Remain completely attentive to what your child is saying. Make eye contact and let your child get everything out.

- Avoid interrupting, even when you have something important to add.

- Reflect back to your child what you heard him say and allow him to add to the story if he wants. Then reflect back again.

- Ask open-ended questions or make statements that invite more from your child. ("Tell me how that makes you feel." "Why don't you want to play with Jason?" "What do you think you should do?")

- Avoid coming to premature conclusions or offering solutions, but rather let your child work on figuring out what to do.

In addition, the most important thing you can offer your child is empathy. This requires a willingness to put yourself in his shoes so your child feels heard in a non-judgmental way.

Empathy is the grace note of active listening, as it allows your child to feel safe, acknowledged, and valued. "It must really hurt your feelings to be left out of a game. I know just how that feels."

Modeling this skill not only helps your child in the moment but also shows him how to use active listening himself. He may not master this skill until he's older (some adults haven't mastered it!), but it will leave a strong impression on how to listen with love and compassion.

In addition to active listening, mindful parenting involves communicating with your preschooler in a way that helps him better understand you and reflects your awareness of your child's stage of development. Your preschooler may push your buttons, irritate you, or even yell at you, but your communication with him must remain calm and steady.

Here are some ways to practice mindful communication with your child:

Use simple language.

Your preschooler has a limited vocabulary and doesn't always understand what you are saying. Use simple and few words to communicate what you want to say or give instructions. Avoid sarcasm, jokes, or indirect statements when trying to communicate something important.

You may want to use more sophisticated language to teach your child new vocabulary, but save this for general conversation when you can explain what you mean. With instructions, consequences, or anything important you want to communicate, be simple, direct, and concise.

Manage your expectations.

Preschoolers are generally egocentric, so don't admonish your child for not understanding another person's viewpoint. Rather, explain how important it is to see things through the eyes and feelings of others. Learning empathy and compassion will be an ongoing lesson for your child.

Also, remember that your child can't understand abstract ideas at this stage, so use concrete examples when you're trying to explain something that involves logic, cause and effect, or reason.

For example, rather than saying, "Don't put too much of the bath bubbles in the tub, or we'll have a big mess on our hands and that will be your responsibility!" say something like, "Only use two squirts of bath bubbles. If we use too much, the bubbles will get big and spill over onto the floor. Then you'll have to clean them up."

Use appropriate non-verbal communication.

Non-verbal communication involves your facial expressions, body language, and tone of voice to reflect your emotions. Children are especially sensitive to non-verbal cues, and it's important that you pay attention to the messages you're sending your child non-verbally.

If you roll your eyes, appear disinterested, or give a particular look, your child will pick up on it and interpret it through his limited understanding of your meaning. Notice what you might be communicating to your child with your non-verbal communication and pay attention to your child's reactions.

Rather than passively expressing yourself with these non-verbal cues, use language that your child can easily understand and won't misinterpret.

Make eye contact.

When you are speaking with your child, look directly at her and make eye contact to show you are interested, engaged, or serious about what you are saying.

Eye contact shows your child that she is important and teaches her to make eye contact with you and others when she is speaking.

Pay attention to your posture and position.

When talking with your child, get down on his level, kneeling or squatting so you can speak to him face-to-face, rather than looming over him so he has to look up at you.

Also, pay attention to the position of your arms and legs. Are you signaling that you're closed off to your child with crossed arms? Do you appear hostile or intimidating? You want your child to feel loved and comforted, even during difficult moments.

Notice your tone of voice.

Do you sound irritated, bored, or distracted? Is your voice harsh and unkind when speaking to your child? Your tone of voice is a powerful communication tool, and preschoolers can often misinterpret what you are saying because of your tone.

Even when you are correcting or disciplining your preschooler, avoid using an overly harsh or unkind tone. You can be serious or even stern, but you don't need to crush your child's spirit with a hurtful tone. Particularly sensitive children can feel shamed and wounded by a negative tone of voice.

Try to maintain a calm, soothing, and soft tone of voice as often as possible so your child feels your love and care even when he has misbehaved. Over time, you'll learn how much "stern" in your voice is necessary to get your child's attention and inspire a behavior change.

Avoid yelling and lecturing.

There will be times when you'll want to yell at your child because your emotions are running high, but this only makes your child fearful of you and teaches her that yelling is an acceptable way to express anger or frustration.

Lecturing your child and droning on about what she has done wrong or why the behavior is bad will make her tune out and stop listening to you. Again, use simple and calm language to communicate what you want to say.

Use touch and facial expressions to show you care.

You can communicate how much you love your child by offering a smile, a wink, or even making a silly face. Offering affection, a pat on the back, or a hand squeeze also communicates how much your child means to you.

Tucking your child in bed at night, tickling him gently, and offering a big hug all give your child the security and comfort of knowing you love him and that he's important to you.

21. Practice Boundary-Based Discipline

Your ability to listen actively and communicate mindfully will serve you well during situations when you need to discipline your preschooler. In fact, both of these skills are essential elements in *boundary-based discipline*.

This type of discipline is grounded in the idea that children behave better when they feel safe and have boundaries.

With this strategy, you communicate clear limits to your child about the boundaries—what's allowed and what isn't. You also clearly communicate the consequences that will occur if your preschooler steps outside of those boundaries. And finally, you consistently follow through with the consequences when your child tests your limits (which most preschoolers tend to do).

Once your child recognizes that you mean what you say, and that you will not allow him to cross your boundary lines, he feels safer and doesn't need to misbehave as often. All of this can be achieved without anger or confusion if you plan in advance and consistently follow through.

In fact, boundary-based discipline is an ideal mindful parenting practice because it incorporates intentionality and forethought, self-awareness and self-control, empathy and love, and natural consequences. You discipline this way to give your child the parameters he needs to be successful, secure, and confident as he moves toward increasing independence.

Here are some ideas for implementing boundary-based discipline strategies with your preschooler.

Determine your house rules.

Sit down with your spouse or partner to develop your list of house rules and the consequences if your child breaks those rules. Think about previous areas of conflict that you want to address, behavior changes you need from your child, and any new boundaries you want to implement.

You don't need to create a list of dozens of rules. Pick your battles and focus on your non-negotiables and priorities.

The following guidelines can help you choose appropriate boundaries and rules for your child:

- Rules related to safety and respect for your home. (For example, no running with scissors or jumping on the furniture.)
- Rules related to respecting the feelings of others. (No name calling or saying hurtful things.)
- Rules related to morality and integrity. (Telling the truth and apologizing when you've done something wrong.)
- Rules related to positive and healthy habits. (Washing your hands after using the bathroom. Putting away your toys after you play with them.)
- Rules related to social skills. (Sharing your toys with your friend. Taking turns on the slide.)
- Rules related to school and life skills. (Finishing your chores before watching TV. Putting some of your allowance in your piggy bank.)

Once you create your list, write down the rules and consequences, and post them where everyone in the family can see them. Only include rules on the list that you intend to follow through on with consequences. You'll need to adjust these rules often as your child grows and you face new behaviors that require boundaries.

Set up a family boundaries meeting.

Ask your child to join you for a special meeting to discuss your family rules and boundaries. Go over this list of rules, presenting them in positive language rather than negative. For example, rather than saying, "Don't yell inside the house," say something like, "Use your indoor voice whenever you are in the house."

Also, offer your child a short explanation for each rule so he'll understand that they aren't just arbitrary but are intended for his well-being and the well-being of others. "We speak kindly to others because in our family we think it's important to treat others just the way we want to be treated."

Once you review the rules, ask for your child's input so he feels invested in the family discourse. He may have ideas related to the rules you present, or he may want to add a few of his own. Take his ideas seriously, include them in the list if they are workable, and discuss alternatives if they aren't.

Discuss possible exceptions to the rules.

Think in advance about times you will make exceptions to any of the rules you devise. For example, you may allow your child to skip a chore if he's feeling ill or let him play outside a little longer on weekend nights.

Talk to your child about what an exception is and how they are special situations—not your regular routine. Let your child know that he can ask about an exception, but that you might not always allow it.

Have high expectations of your child.

The Pygmalion effect[47] is a phenomenon in which people perform to the standards of the expectations held for them by others. It's supported by a study by psychologists Robert Rosenthal and Lenore Jacobson that showed how students' performances were enhanced when teachers expected high performances from them.

If you expect your child to honor the boundaries you've established, and you clearly communicate your expectations, your child is more likely to behave accordingly. In fact, research[48] confirms that children whose parents have high (but reasonable) expectations of them are more likely to be successful in life.

If you want to reinforce your positive expectations for your child about your rules and boundaries, create a guided visualization that you can practice with her related to successfully managing a behavioral challenge or boundary. As part of the visualization, include a scene in which you and your partner praise your child for her behavior and others comment on her skills.

Give warnings when possible.

Help your child be successful at honoring your family boundaries by offering a warning in situations that could lead to conflict. For example, if your child has been playing outside with friends and needs to come inside to wash up before dinner, let her know five to ten minutes in advance that she'll need to end her playtime and come inside in a few minutes.

---

47   https://en.wikipedia.org/wiki/Pygmalion_effect
48   https://psycnet.apa.org/record/2007-01726-011

You can also offer "if-then" warnings in the moment that remind your child that his choices have consequences. "You can come inside now and wash up for dinner or stay outside longer and lose your playtime with Sarah tomorrow." Giving your child a choice teaches him that his decisions can result in positive or negative consequences.

When your child slips up and forgets a rule, there are times when it may seem more appropriate to offer one warning (just one). "Sit down, Jason. You know the rule about jumping on the bed." Just don't allow warnings to become your consistent form of discipline. Lecturing without consequences just becomes noise to your child over time.

Some infractions call for immediate consequences with no warning. This is the best way to get your child's attention and remind him how serious you are about the importance of this rule. "I told you never to leave the scissors on the floor because the baby can get hurt. You can't use the scissors for the rest of the week, and you need to sit in time-out right now."

Use logical consequences.

Try your best to make the punishment fit the crime. If your child doesn't put his toys away after using them, then he loses the privilege of playing with them the next day. Natural consequences help your child learn personal responsibility and mentally cement the boundaries so he doesn't have to experience the consequences again.

In the book *Parenting with Love and Logic*,[49] authors Foster Cline and Jim Fay suggest that natural consequences are part of a loving approach to discipline:

> Effective parenting centers around love: love that is not permissive, love that doesn't tolerate disrespect, but also love that is powerful enough to allow kids to make mistakes and permit them to live with the consequences of those mistakes.

When a child must deal with the consequences of his actions, he learns to think for himself and eventually recognizes why certain behaviors are unacceptable. You may want to protect your child from the pain of natural consequences, but they are the best way to help him develop personal responsibility.

Every situation may not present natural consequences that are obvious or immediate enough to be effective. You may need to get creative with your consequences, but try your best to make them relate to the misbehavior in some way.

If your child has hurt someone's feelings, broken something that belongs to someone else, or done anything that merits an apology, make sure the apology happens as quickly as possible, ideally in person.

Practice consistency.

Consistency is the foundation of boundary-based discipline. If you don't follow through with enforcing your rules, you may as well not set them. In fact, not following through or making regular exceptions can make behavior problems even worse

---

49 https://www.amazon.com/Parenting-Love-Logic-Teaching-Responsibility-ebook/dp/B00IV351R0

because you're sending mixed messages that are confusing to your preschooler.

When your child sees and believes that you follow through with your rules, she will see you as a predictable leader who provides consistency, security, and safety—something your preschooler craves. Unpredictability causes anxiety in children and can lead to hostility, aggression, or complacency.

Use mindful discernment.

Mindful parenting and boundary-based discipline should work hand-in-hand. Your goal isn't to gain robot-like compliance from your child in every situation. Your goal is to teach your child appropriate and safe behaviors while remaining fluid and aware of the situation at hand.

As you practice boundary-based discipline, maintain a sense of mindful discernment in which you constantly asked yourself, "What is needed most in this moment?" Many times, a consistent consequence is the needed action.

But there are times when you need to recognize the variables at play when your child crosses the line. Maybe he's tired or insecure. Maybe he needs to feel autonomous or empowered in some way.

It's hard to be discerning in a tense moment when you feel angry or embarrassed. But take a deep breath and give yourself time to be fully present with the moment and what's happening. Don't miss an opportunity for empathy, compassion, or love when it's needed—even if a consequence is inevitable.

Be a good role model.

Only include rules on your list that you can honor yourself. Your child needs to see that you are practicing what you preach and that you follow through on the rules as well. If you're requiring your child to speak kindly to others but you and your spouse speak unkindly to each other, you're sending your child a conflicting message.

If you do break a family rule (like using your smartphone at the dinner table), own your mistake, acknowledge that your child is right (if he pointed out the infraction), and apologize. Then try harder not to break the rule.

There will be times when you have a legitimate and important reason to break the house rules. You might break the "no phones at the dinner table" rule because an important call is coming in from the doctor. Or you might leave your papers scattered on the floor because you haven't had time to organize them before putting them away.

Explain to your preschooler that you are an adult and that adults understand when it's necessary to break a rule, especially when it relates to important adult matters. But thank your preschooler for reminding you of the rules and let him know you'll do your best to stick to them, just as he does.

Boundary-based discipline gives you and your child the security of knowing what to expect from each other within the framework that you've established and discussed as a family. It gives you both the space to enjoy your relationship and family life without fretting about expectations or what to do when behavioral situations arise.

Your child may test you at first, but with consistent responses from you, coupled with mindful discernment, your preschooler will feel secure and loved knowing that you have things under control.

22. Delay Digital Interactions

Your children's generation will be among the first to have never known life without digital devices (smartphones, tablets, and computers). Technology has become a ubiquitous part of our daily lives, so much so that we see these devices in the hands of children who aren't yet out of diapers.

In fact, researchers[50] at the University of Iowa discovered that by age two, 90% of children had a moderate ability to use a tablet. Says Dr. Fran Walfish, a Los Angeles-based child and family psychotherapist in an article for the blog Little Things,[51] "We have a lot of 2-year-olds using tablets now, and I see 3- and 4-year-olds that are already addicted."

As your preschooler grows older, it will become much harder to limit the time she spends on digital devices. Tablets and smartphones have edged their way into classrooms and day cares across the country, and they likely will be used by most of her peers during non-school hours.

But during these preschool years, you have more control over whether or not your child uses technology and, if so, for how long. As a mindful parent, you should use this control wisely. A preschooler really doesn't *need* technology for anything. Nor will she have access to these devices unless you allow it.

Rather than handing your child a device to keep her busy or to provide entertainment, take a moment to recognize exactly what happens to your child when she spends time on them and how this early usage can impact her development.

---

50 https://now.uiowa.edu/2015/06/how-do-toddlers-use-tablets
51 https://www.littlethings.com/reasons-not-to-give-children-technology/

Because these digital devices have become mainstream only in the last decade or so, their long-term effects on childhood development and growth are still not fully realized. But the available information we have to date is already confirming that the use of them by young children should be carefully monitored, if not avoided altogether.

We suggest you delay this access as long as possible, and here's why:

There's an addictive quality to these devices.

Kids' brains undergo neurobiological changes when they regularly use technology. Once in your child's hands, a tablet or smartphone is hard to put down. The sensory seductions are too strong for a little one to resist.

Because he is immediately rewarded (with entertainment, messages, etc.) at the click of a button, your child's brain is being rewired to crave this immediate gratification.

His brain is secreting the neurotransmitter dopamine (a feel-good chemical), which activates the reward pathways in the brain. Of course, your child wants to keep feeling the good feelings provided by these devices. But as a result, he doesn't learn patience, moderation, or impulse control.

With frequent use of digital devices, children aren't challenged to find creative ways to entertain themselves or find solutions to problems when they can easily obtain what they need with a device.

They can trigger power struggles and "tech tantrums."

You may have noticed how children using these devices in restaurants, airplanes, and other public places stare at them with glazed eyes, lost in a drug-like virtual world.

Pulling your preschooler away from a device can quickly turn into a power struggle between the two of you. Your child won't easily disengage from the games or shows that he's become attached to.

When you force him to disengage, not only are you terminating the dopamine supply that these devices trigger, you're also interrupting the psychological flow state that occurs when he's engrossed in a game or show.

Taking away a device when your child is so absorbed can result in a full-blown meltdown. And if you hand your child a device to "calm him down" during or after a tantrum, you're just reinforcing this bad behavior.

They can negatively impact your child's sleep.

Many children take these devices to bed with them, playing games and watching shows without supervision. Not only will a child resist sleep in order to spend time on a device, but the device can make it more difficult to fall asleep.

The blue light that emits from a screen suppresses the sleep hormone melatonin and changes the body's natural sleep-wake cycle. This results in a sleep-deprived child who doesn't have the energy to play outside or manage emotions the next day. Then parents are tempted to deal with the fallout by allowing more screen time. It becomes a vicious cycle.

They can affect your child's ability to learn.

Regular use of these digital devices can lead to distractibility that can contribute to poor academic performance once your preschooler is in school. A new Canadian study[52] confirms that too much screen time for preschoolers is connected with developmental delays and a lack of school readiness.

Says Jenny Radesky, MD, clinical instructor in developmental-behavioral pediatrics at Boston University,[53] "These devices also may replace the hands-on activities important for the development of sensorimotor and visual-motor skills, which are important for the learning and application of math and science."

Time on these devices can also impact your preschooler's critical thinking, problem-solving, ability to focus, and social skills—abilities that should be developed through exploring, unstructured play, and interacting with peers. When they are constantly distracted with devices, children aren't using their imaginations or learning how to interact with others.

They can lead to obesity.

If a child is frequently using digital devices, he is less likely to spend time outdoors getting the necessary exercise to maintain a healthy body. Limited physical activity leads to weight gain.

A variety of studies[54] have found a direct correlation between screen media exposure and increased risks of obesity in children. This is not only due to lack of physical exercise, but also because kids are eating more junk foods while on these devices and getting less sleep.

52   https://jamanetwork.com/journals/jamapediatrics/article-abstract/2722666
53   https://www.eurekalert.org/pub_releases/2015-01/bumc-mai013015.php
54   https://www.ncbi.nlm.nih.gov/pmc/articles/PMC5769928/

As your child grows older, there will be additional issues to confront related to digital devices, including cyberbullying, mental health problems, social anxiety, and aggression. Technology has changed the way kids socialize and interact with others, and that can have a profound impact on their mental and emotional well-being. For both kids and adults, excessive social media use can lower self-esteem and trigger negative moods.

Now, we aren't suggesting that technology has no value for your children. Technology provides many positive opportunities for learning, entertainment, and socializing. But preschool-aged children have years ahead of them to take advantage of these benefits.

While they are young, their education and socialization should come from real-world activities that involve face-to-face interactions, creative play, and lots of time outside. They need to learn how to find antidotes to their boredom, entertain themselves without devices, and make friends they can see and touch.

You may not choose to completely ban these devices from your preschooler, but if you decide to allow them, be intentional about when and how much your preschooler uses them.

The American Academy of Pediatrics (AAP) recommends limiting the amount of time that preschoolers spend in front of a screen to one to two hours a day. This recommendation includes TV shows in addition to streaming videos, games or apps, and websites.

In retrospect, Barrie wishes she had limited the amount of TV time she allowed for her kids when they were preschoolers. Even though her children didn't have access to smartphones or tablets until they were preteens, she recognizes that much of the

TV time allowed when they were young was more for her benefit and convenience than for her children's well-being.

After a long day working or tending to children, parents are understandably tempted to hand over a device just for some much-needed peace and quiet. But remember, if you allow these devices, it can be a slippery slope toward conflict and meltdowns (and some of the other problems listed previously) if you don't set some ground rules and monitor your child's usage.

Consider the following strategies.

Create your own family media plan.

Sit down with your spouse or partner and decide together what your family media plan will be. You may want to read through the remainder of this section before you answer the following questions to help you come up with a plan.

- Which devices will you allow your child to use (TV, smartphone, computer, tablet)?
- How many hours a day is your child allowed to watch TV and/or use a device?
- What are those hours?
- Where in your house is your child allowed to use the devices?
- Do you need to be present when your child is using them?
- Where and when are devices never allowed?
- Is your child allowed to use devices in the car, at a restaurant, or in other public places? If so, what are your rules about these occasions?
- How will you monitor what your child is seeing or watching?

- How will you let your child know it's time to stop using a device?

Communicate your family rules about devices.

Have a family meeting with your preschooler to talk about your rules related to TV time and use of digital devices. Explain to your child why you have these rules and how too much time in front of a screen can make your brain sick, just like too much candy can make your tummy sick.

Discuss your family values and how you prioritize time spent on activities that are better for his emotional, physical, mental, and social development. "Mom and I believe it's much better for you and our family if we spend more time outside and with our friends and family."

Write down the rules, even though your child can't read them, and post them on the refrigerator or another place that's visible to everyone. This visible cue will remind your child of the rules you've discussed.

Monitor your preschooler's use.

Don't allow unstructured, unsupervised use of digital devices by your preschooler. Your young child could easily stumble onto something that is inappropriate or even dangerous. Make sure that you help choose and approve the games, apps, programs, and software she is engaging with.

Be sure to do your homework so you know whether or not the media your child sees are indeed educational and appropriate.

Visit Common Sense Media[55] to find reviews of age-appropriate apps and programs.

Join your child as she engages with digital devices.

Yes, the benefit for you when your child is using a device or watching television is that you get a break to do what you need to do without interruption. But don't always let your child play or watch alone.

Co-view and co-engage with your child when she is online to encourage social interaction and learning. If you're playing a digital game together, you can demonstrate sportsmanlike conduct if you win or lose. You can discuss an educational program together and share your reactions or explain something your child isn't clear about.

Children are often far ahead of their parents when it comes to understanding and enjoying the games and programs on these devices. Participate with your child and let her show you the ropes so that you have something to bond over and talk about.

Plan for easy tech transitions.

If you want to avoid the "tech tantrums," be proactive in planning a transition that helps your preschooler detach from the digital dopamine rush so he can move on to the next activity or event of the day.

For example, if you allow your child thirty minutes to use his favorite app on your phone, consider setting a timer for twenty-five minutes. When that timer goes off, remind your child he

---

55   https://www.commonsensemedia.org

has five minutes left to play, and set the timer again for five minutes.

Once the final timer goes off, transition your child to something pleasurable (his favorite snack, a game with you, a walk to the park, etc.) so that the dopamine supply isn't totally withdrawn when he stops using the device.

Asking your child to transition from screen time to cleaning his room or going to a doctor's appointment is more likely to cause a meltdown than offering a pleasurable activity first.

Be a good digital role model.

Try to limit or manage your own time on these devices so that you're a good role model for your child. If you bring the phone to the dinner table or don't look up from your computer while talking to your child, he will surely mimic your behavior.

Of course, it's fine to let your child know that adults need these devices for work and other uses that aren't necessary for kids. Your brain is fully formed, and you can make executive decisions about yourself and your digital habits.

But as often as possible, show your child that you prefer real-world interactions and activities. Try to limit your smartphone and computer usage to times when little eyes aren't watching you.

Be consistent with your rules.

There will be times when you'll be tempted to break the digital rules you've set for your child, and sometimes breaking your rules makes more sense than enforcing them. But the more inconsistent you are, the more difficult it will be to enforce the rules when you want to.

If your child begs to use a device, and you give in because you're tired and don't want to deal with the whining, then you're sending the message that you aren't serious about your guidelines.

But there may be a time when allowing your child to use a device (outside of the normal timeframes you've devised) makes sense. For example, maybe you're in a busy waiting room at the doctor's office and there's nothing for your child to do.

In these cases, tell your child why you are making an exception, and that this is a one-off situation—not the new normal. But even if you've grown inconsistent with your digital rules (as all parents do from time to time), you can have another family meeting to discuss implementing the rules again.

Have a plan for tech tantrums.

Decide in advance how you will handle the situation if your child does have a meltdown when tech time is over. If you catch the meltdown early, you may be able to calm it quickly by distracting your child with something she enjoys doing. Or you might need to remind your child that if she has a tantrum, she won't be able to use the device at all the next day.

In fact, a tantrum might be a signal that your child is too attached to technology and needs a break from it anyway. Talk to your child about this and explain why you need to put the devices away for a few days. Then reintroduce them for shorter and less frequent amounts of time.

If the tantrum has quickly moved from zero to a hundred and your preschooler is totally losing it, spending some time in her room to calm down is your best immediate option. You can have a calm conversation later about why you need to enforce a digital break for a few days or a week.

192

23. Encourage and Support Your Preschooler's Independence

Many tantrums for both toddlers and preschoolers are triggered by the child's inability to do something he wants to do—put on shoes, climb the monkey bars, or use scissors, for example. Toddlers may be frustrated because they are physically or mentally unable to accomplish a task or activity or because you're preventing them from doing something that might be dangerous.

Preschoolers feel the same frustrations, but now they are developmentally ready to do more on their own—from using the potty to riding a bike (with training wheels). But their readiness must be primed by your willingness to teach them these skills.

Unless your child is in day care or preschool, it's up to you to help her learn what she is ready and eager to learn. Yes, this will take time and patience on your part, but your efforts will result in a happier, more independent child.

You'll experience fewer tantrums and power struggles when your child can do things for herself rather than depending on you to do them for her. She will feel more confident and competent stretching her cognitive and physical abilities and successfully managing basic life and developmental skills for herself.

Says Amy McCready, a child discipline expert and founder of Positive Parenting Solutions, in an article for Parents.com,[56] "The most important thing to work on is training. If we take the time to teach them how to do things, from personal care to helping

---

56   https://www.parents.com/toddlers-preschoolers/development/behavioral
/preschoolers-101-understanding-preschooler-development/

with dinner, they will feel more empowered and less likely to act out. The more time we spend on training, the less time we have to spend on correcting negative behavior."

If you're not completely sure what your preschooler is capable of doing, let's take a look at some of the typical skills and chores you can expect for three-, four-, and five-year-olds.

Most three-year-olds are able to do the following:

- Run and walk easily
- Jump, hop, and stand on one foot
- Walk up and down stairs using one foot on each step
- Walk backward
- Kick and throw a small ball (and catch a bigger ball most of the time)
- Start pedaling a tricycle or bike
- Draw a circle
- Play with toys with small moving parts and buttons
- Turn the pages of a book one at a time
- Build with blocks and create towers of six or more blocks
- Work door handles and twist-on bottle tops
- Name the eight colors in a crayon box (red, yellow, blue, green, orange, purple, brown, black)
- Recite numbers to ten (but may not understand counting)
- Sort objects by shape and color
- Begin to understand time in terms of morning, night, and days of the week
- Remember and retell favorite stories

- Understand things that are the "same" and "different"
- Follow commands with two- or three-step directions ("Put away the game. Wash your hands. Come sit down for dinner.")

Most four-year-olds are able to:

- Start, stop, turn, and go around obstacles while running
- Do somersaults, skip, and trot
- Get dressed with minimal help (zippers, snaps, and buttons may still be a little hard)
- Brush teeth and wash face
- Throw and bounce a ball (and throw overhand)
- Jump over objects
- Climb playground ladders
- Pedal and steer a tricycle or bike
- Draw or copy basic shapes and crosses
- Stack a tower at least ten blocks high
- String beads to make necklaces
- Pinch and shape clay or play-dough into recognizable objects
- Write some letters
- Understand counting and count ten or more objects
- Understand the concepts of "same" and "different"
- Begin to use scissors purposefully
- Draw a person with a body

Most five-year-olds are able to:

- Walk on tiptoes and walk heel-to-toe (like on a balance beam)
- Jump rope
- Pump legs to swing
- Stand and hop on each foot
- Catch softball-sized ball
- Move in different ways at the same time to do things (like swim, dribble a basketball, or dance)
- Practice hand dominance, using one hand more than the other
- Hold a pencil using a tripod grip (two fingers and a thumb)
- Cut basic shapes with scissors; possibly cut a straight line
- Use a fork, spoon, and knife easily
- Wipe and wash after using the bathroom
- Recognize and name colors and basic shapes
- Know the letters of the alphabet and their sounds
- Know and recite name, address, and phone number
- Understand basic concepts about reading print (which way the pages go and how words are read left to right and top to bottom)
- Know that stories have a beginning, middle, and end
- Count groups of objects up to ten and recite numbers to twenty
- Stick with an activity for fifteen minutes and finish a short project

- Make plans about how to play, what to build, or what to draw

How to Teach Developmental Skills

Some of these skills your child may develop independently (climbing, jumping, stacking, for example), but you will need to teach him or help him refine most of these skills during the preschool years.

When teaching or helping your child learn developmental skills, you may need to carve out some time during the day to play "school" with him if he isn't in a formal preschool program.

Much of your child's learning will occur naturally through play and typical interactions with family and friends. But you can set up your own learning center in your home and create a simple curriculum of fun activities to support his developing mental, physical, and social abilities.

These activities don't have to be a formal academic program or homeschool curriculum. You want your preschooler to see these activities as fun and exciting, not rigorous and demanding.

As a mindful parent, pay attention to the way your child learns and what sparks his curiosity. Focus your teaching efforts to support your child's learning style or styles. Your child may learn best in one or more of the following ways:

- Visual (spatial): Preferring pictures, images, and spatial understanding
- Aural (auditory-musical): Preferring sound and music
- Verbal (linguistic): Preferring words in speech and writing

- Physical (kinesthetic): Preferring to use the body, hands, and sense of touch

- Logical (mathematical): Preferring logic, reasoning, and systems

- Social (interpersonal): Preferring to learn in groups or with other people

- Solitary (intrapersonal): Preferring to work alone with self-study

As you discover the way your child learns, tailor a weekly schedule for your preschooler that includes some mix of the following:

- Short activities related to learning letters, numbers, colors, and shapes

- Short science and nature activities, both indoors and outside

- Tactile activities to teach fine motor skills (stringing beads, working puzzles, etc.)

- Life skill lessons (setting the table, personal hygiene, learning address and phone number, etc.)

- Reading time when you read to your preschooler

- Creative and artistic play (where you instruct or assist with cutting, gluing, etc. as necessary)

- Music time for music appreciation, movement, or playing an instrument

- Outdoor play that involves throwing, catching, climbing, balancing, etc.

You'll find hundreds of resources online to help you decide how to set up your in-home learning environment and choose appropriate activities. This list of forty preschool activities[57] is a good place to start. Also, check out "preschool activities" on Pinterest for more ideas and printables you can download.

Chores for Preschoolers

In addition to learning these developmental skills, your preschooler is also capable of taking on several household chores. Giving your child chores and teaching him how to perform them the right way gives him a sense of competence and importance within the family.

Most preschoolers are keen observers and want to emulate you. They are enthusiastic about helping, maybe more so than at any other age, and will often plead to assist you with chores—even those they aren't ready to handle. But there are plenty of chores they can perform well.

Your preschooler can handle any of these chores:
- Pulling up the bed
- Putting folded clothes in drawers
- Putting dirty clothes in a hamper
- Picking up toys and tidying the bedroom
- Putting shoes away
- Bringing in bags of groceries
- Helping put away groceries
- Preparing simple snacks

57 https://thestay-at-home-momsurvivalguide.com/40-activities-for-prescho ol-at-home/

- Setting the table
- Taking dishes to the sink
- Filling a pet bowl
- Wiping up messes
- Dusting
- Sorting laundry
- Matching socks
- Putting away clean utensils
- Watering plants
- Helping with a garden
- Helping with meal preparation
- Emptying trash cans
- Getting the mail
- Helping clean the car
- Picking up pinecones or outdoor debris

Teaching your child how to properly complete chores can happen naturally when you are about to tackle a particular chore, or you can set aside a specific time to talk about chores and work on them with your child. Here are some important suggestions to consider when setting up chores for your preschooler:

- Discuss with your child why chores are important for each family member and how they benefit the entire family.

- Create a weekly chore chart (with a picture for each chore if your child can't read), or download this chart[58] from the

___

58   https://drive.google.com/file/d/0BzGWZ-5egKbUVnFmTTZncVVMa Tg/edit

site "Hey There, Home." Post the chart where your child can see what he needs to do each day.

- Talk with your child about performing chores mindfully, paying attention to the details of each action, and feeling gratitude for the benefits related to the chore. For example, remind your child to feel grateful for a comfortable bed when he is making it up.

- Set up a structure for your child's daily chores that's predictable and consistent. Consider chore times for the morning and evening that your child can expect every day.

- Praise your child's efforts even if they aren't perfect. A preschooler craves this reinforcement and positive feedback from you.

- Create a reward system for your child for completing chores. This might be a gold star or sticker on a chore chart, or some physical reward like a small allowance.

- Don't allow special privileges (electronics or playtime) until chores are completed.

- Don't use chores as a punishment for misbehavior. Chores should be considered a normal part of daily life (even though they aren't always pleasant for children). The more negativity you associate with chores, the harder it will be to get your child to comply with them.

Teaching your child skills that encourage independence not only helps his confidence and emotional reactivity, but also prepares him for the demands of school and life that await.

As a mindful parent, you make the conscious choice to work with your preschooler on these skills with patience and love, knowing that the short-term sacrifice of your time and energy is essential for your child's well-being. Your efforts also reflect your family values of intentionality, personal responsibility, and cooperation—values that your child will hopefully emulate throughout his life.

24. Turn Mindfulness into Games for Your Preschooler

Preschool children have vivid imaginations and practice creative visualization and mindfulness without even knowing they are doing so. Especially if you've limited television time and technology, your child's mind is busily engaged in the world around him and in his interior world of daydreams, make-believe play, and creative ideas.

For most young children, being mindful is their natural state of being, before they become distracted by the demands of modern life. That's why it's so important to allow your child plenty of unstructured time for play and outdoor activity so that he can foster that state of oneness with himself and his activities.

This state of flow and oneness that children naturally possess is the desired state adults seek to achieve during meditation and other mindfulness practices. As your child grows older, he'll be pulled further and further away from this unique and wondrous time when he can engage in a near constant state of present moment awareness.

As a parent, you can reinforce and celebrate your child's natural sense of presence by introducing the concept of mindfulness and teaching him how to practice it through games and fun activities.

You can provide a foundational understanding that mindfulness provides an anchor to inner peace, contentment, and happiness—feelings that become increasingly diluted during the school age years and beyond. Your child can turn to these activities whenever he feels emotional turmoil or frustration to find composure and self-control.

Preschoolers are at the perfect age to learn and enjoy mindfulness activities. They are old enough to have the attention span (and desire) to learn and practice them, and young enough to engage in them with willingness and joy.

Many of the mindfulness games and activities we outlined in the toddler section are also applicable for preschoolers, and if you've introduced mindfulness activities to your toddler, you're ahead of the game. But if you haven't yet introduced your child to mindfulness practices, we hope you'll make them a part of your daily schedule with your preschooler.

Let's look at some additional games and activities that teach mindfulness skills that your preschooler is sure to enjoy.

Guided Visualization Game

This is a fun game for a rainy day or before bed to stoke your child's imagination and help her create mental pictures of things she wants to do, places she wants to go, feelings she needs to deal with, or a goal she wants to achieve.

Visualization is simply creating mental pictures or imagery in great detail. It helps your child imagine positive and healing experiences to develop coping skills and master new behaviors and skills.

As we explain in our book *10-Minute Mindfulness*,[59] visualization is an incredibly powerful tool with so many benefits.

---

59 https://www.amazon.com/10-Minute-Mindfulness-Habits-Living-Present-ebook/dp/B071HVMVVR

It can be used in daily life to relieve stress and performance anxiety, enhance preparation, and add more power to your physical and mental efforts.

Visualization has been shown to impact motor control, attention, perception, planning, and memory, priming your brain for success in whatever you want to accomplish.

Simply the act of visualizing, which requires mindfulness, focus, and creativity, frees the mind from mental chatter and negativity.

By using visualization, you create strong neural pathways in your brain, just as if you had actually performed what you visualize. Because the brain tells the muscles how to move, these neural pathways result in more precise, stronger movements, enhancing your actual efforts.

You can guide your child through the visualization process either with a scene or topic that you devise, or one that your child wants to focus on. The guided imagery you practice could be:

- Related to a problem or fear your child has recently experienced, and a way to resolve it (like feeling left out, fear about strangers, etc.).

- A new skill your child is working on, and all of the steps involved in mastering the skill (like riding a bike or jumping rope).

- A beautiful setting that is calming and relaxing for your child, that she chooses or you devise.

- A story you tell in which your child is the main character and you are teaching a lesson or helping her with a challenge.

Says writer Patti Teel for the site Pathways to Family Wellness,[60] "We help our children to create their own experiences by encouraging them to visualize or imagine themselves obtaining their heart's desire. By imagining that they already have what they desire, children will allow it and welcome it into their reality. Pure desire is a wonderful thing: it is a feeling of expectation and anticipation."

You'll likely be able to create your guided imagery script on the fly, but if you have some specific elements you want to include, write down bullet points so you'll remember them.

To begin the game, tell your child that you have a fun game to play together called "The Imagination Game" (or some other clever name you come up with). Then follow these steps:

- Ask your child to sit in a chair or cross-legged on the floor with his hands resting in his lap.

- Have him close his eyes as you count backward from ten to one while your child takes a breath with each count.

- Begin the guided visualization with present tense words like, "You are now opening the gate that leads into a secret garden." Continue to speak in the present tense, as though your child is actively experiencing or participating in whatever you are describing.

- Use as much detail as possible, drawing on as many of your child's senses as possible—sight, sound, taste, touch, and smell. "You feel the rough wood as the gate squeaks open and immediately notice the bright colors of hundreds of flowers and trees in full bloom. You hear birds singing and

60 https://pathwaystofamilywellness.org/Inspirational/the-power-of-a-childs -imagination.html

water splashing in a nearby creek. Then you notice a swing that's just your size hanging from a tree."

- If you're helping your child with a particular skill, like riding a bike, go into as much detail as possible, using words that suggest your child is accomplishing each element of the skill. For example: "You sit on your bike, push off with one foot, and begin peddling with the other. You start peddling with both feet, balancing perfectly as you ride down the sidewalk in front of our house. You feel the breeze in your hair and feel so proud as Mom and Dad watch you."

- Once you finish the guided visualization, ask your child to breathe again as you count up from one to ten.

- When your child opens his eyes, discuss the guided imagery and what he felt and noticed. Ask questions about his favorite part and what felt the most real to him. Did his mind wander or stay with the imagery? What would he have added to the scene or story?

- You might consider recording several guided visualizations for your child to use on his own whenever he wants to enjoy this mindfulness experience. A recorded sleep visualization is a soothing way to help your child fall asleep. But don't neglect to practice these guided imagery sessions together at times, as the practice is both a bonding and mindfulness experience for you and your child. Here are a couple of guided imagery scripts you can use.[61]

---

61 https://www.themindfulword.org/2012/guided-imagery-scripts-children
-anxiety-stress/

The Mindfulness Jar

This simple but profound mindfulness activity helps your pre-schooler understand the connection between her feelings of stress and worry and an overactive mind. With this game, you'll teach her how to calm her mind in order to feel better.

To create the mindfulness jar, you'll need:

- A glass jar and lid (with no labels on the jar)
- 2 tbsp of glitter glue (a color that you can easily see in water)
- Warm water (enough to partially fill the jar)

Set these items out with your child and explain that you're going to show her what it's like when her mind is filled with lots of thoughts and strong emotions. Discuss how fearful, angry, and sad thoughts can make negative feelings seem overwhelming but that you are going to show her how to be in charge of her thoughts so that feelings aren't so overwhelming.

Pour the warm water into the jar and add the glitter glue. Put the lid on the jar and let your child shake it up really fast—something she'll love doing. Then watch all of the glitter swirl around in the water in a crazy, mixed-up way.

Explain that the water is her mind and the glitter is all of her thoughts. When the glitter (or her thoughts) swirls around, the water (her mind) is turbulent and upset.

Then, as the water settles and the glitter floats to the bottom of the jar, ask your child to be very still and practice deep and calm breathing until all of the glitter and water is settled.

Talk about the connection between stillness and focused breathing and calming your mind. Teach your child that whenever the "glitter" in her mind gets too shaken up, she can calm herself by sitting still, closing her eyes, and practicing breathing.

The visual reminder of the glitter in the swirling water helps your preschooler remember that she has the power within herself to calm her thoughts and feelings, even without the mindfulness jar.

But the mindfulness jar itself also helps by being a physical outlet to release energy in a way that is less destructive than punching, smacking, or kicking.

While your child holds the bottle and watches the glitter settle, her hands and eyes will be brought to the middle of the jar, which helps center the nervous system. The slow descent of the glitter in the jar acts as a visual model that even unconsciously helps slow her heart rate and breathing.

Talk about your own experiences with strong feelings and the thoughts that cause them. Let your child know that you use breathing to calm your mind and ease your emotions. Tell your child that this is a practice you use regularly and that it will help her for the rest of her life.

Focus and Balance Game

This game helps your child remain focused, present, and attentive while trying to balance a boiled egg on a spoon. Your child learns to direct his attention to a task that requires some amount of coordination, balance, and calm in order to succeed— something your preschooler loves to do!

Here's how to prepare for and play the game:

- Boil several eggs (in case it takes several attempts) and let them cool down.

- Once the eggs are cool, grab a spoon and one of the eggs. Instruct your child that he will have to balance the egg on the spoon while slowly walking a course you define.

- For younger preschoolers, this might be walking a straight line for five to ten steps. For older children, you might create an obstacle course to walk around, or just make the length of the straight line longer.

- Allow your child to practice a few steps balancing the egg on the spoon in order to get the feel of it. Remind your child that he has to watch the egg and spoon carefully to ensure it doesn't fall off. He also needs to walk slowly so that the egg remains balanced.

- Once your child successfully follows the course without dropping the egg, you can encourage him to go faster, or you can make the course slightly more difficult.

When you finish the game, talk with your child about where his mind was while walking and trying to balance the egg. If he drops the egg, ask him what happened that made him drop it. Was it because he got distracted and didn't focus?

Talk about how important it is to be focused on a task without giving in to distractions in order to be successful. Also discuss how it feels to be so focused. For most of us, it is enjoyable to be so intently focused on a task because it is calming and puts us in the state of flow, where time seems to disappear.

This may be a hard concept for a preschooler to understand, but you can begin to reinforce the positive aspects of paying attention when engaged in a task, even if the task isn't fun.

Pebble Meditation

This meditation activity for children is inspired by the teachings of Vietnamese monk and spiritual leader Thich Nhat Hanh. He writes about it in his book for children, *A Handful of Quiet: Happiness in Four Pebbles.*[62]

This meditation teaches the four qualities of happiness: beauty/freshness, stability/solidity, peace/tranquility, and freedom/liberation. It is a fun and tangible way to introduce meditation and to talk about what it really means to be happy.

The ritual and routine of this meditation will engage and delight your child. But over time and with practice, your child will also look forward to the feelings of calm and happiness that result from this practice.

Here's how to practice this meditation activity with your preschooler:

- Go on a "rock hunt" with your child to find four rocks to use for the meditation. Smooth river rocks are ideal, but any small rocks or pebbles that fit easily into your child's hand will work. Find four rocks for yourself as well.

- Each pebble represents either a flower, a mountain, water, or space—and each has a specific quality, as mentioned above.

---

62   https://www.amazon.com/Handful-Quiet-Happiness-Four-Pebbles-ebook/dp/B00APDASFY

- Put the pebbles in a pouch (like a small jewelry pouch) or a small box without a lid. You'll need a separate pouch for you and your child.

- If the weather is nice, find a quiet spot outside for the meditation. If not, find a quiet space in your home that is free from distractions.

- Sit across from your child and have him place his pouch of pebbles on the left-hand side of his body, close enough to reach. You do the same with your pouch.

- Ask your child to take three slow, deep breaths, and you do the same.

- Ask your child to pick up the first stone with his left hand and move it to his right hand. Then both of you should close your eyes.

- As you both hold the pebbles in your right hands, speak the following words while inhaling: "Breathing in, I am a flower." On the exhale say, "Breathing out, I am fresh."

- Over the next three cycles of inhales and exhales, quietly whisper, "flower" on the inhale and "fresh" on the exhale.

- After the last cycle, both of you should put the pebbles down on the right sides of your bodies.

- Next ask your child to pick up the second stone with his left hand and move it to his right hand.

- As you both hold the pebbles in your right hands, speak the following words while inhaling: "Breathing in, I see myself as a mountain." On the exhale say, "Breathing out, I am solid."

- Over the next three cycles of inhales and exhales, quietly whisper, "mountain" on the inhale and "solid" on the exhale.

- Then put the pebbles down on the right sides of your bodies.

- Now ask your child to pick up the third stone with his left hand and move it to his right hand.

- As you both hold the pebbles in your right hands, speak the following words while inhaling: "Breathing in, I see myself as still, clear water." On the exhale say, "Breathing out, I reflect things as they are."

- Over the next three cycles of inhales and exhales, quietly whisper "clear water" on the inhale and "reflecting" on the exhale.

- Then put the pebbles down on the right sides of your bodies.

- Finally, ask your child to pick up the fourth stone with his left hand and move it to his right hand.

- As you both hold the pebbles in your right hands, speak the following words while inhaling: "Breathing in, I see myself as space." On the exhale the practitioner says, "Breathing out, I am free."

- Over the next three cycles of inhales and exhales, quietly whisper, "space" on the inhale and "free" on the exhale.

- Then put the pebbles down on the right sides of your bodies.

You may need to go through this meditation yourself one time in front of your child to show him exactly what to do. Then you can do it together once your child knows what to do.

As he becomes comfortable with the practice, your preschooler can use the pebbles as tangible objects to hold for comfort and calm whenever he feels upset or agitated.

If you need to alter the wording slightly to make it more understandable or relatable for your child, feel free to do so. For example, if your child doesn't understand the word "reflect," you can say something like, "Breathing out, I am a mirror."

25. Slow Down and Do Less

If you want your children to turn out well, spend twice as much time with them, and half as much money. —Abigail van Buren

When Barrie was a child, she didn't go to preschool. In the early 1960s, when she was preschool age, only 10%[63] of the nation's three- and four-year-olds were enrolled in a classroom setting. Today, the vast majority of preschool-aged children are enrolled in some kind of public or private preschool program, according to K12 Academics.

> By 2005, 69 percent, or over 800,000, four-year-old children nationwide participated in some type of state preschool program. The yearly increase in enrollment of preschool programs throughout the years is due to an increase of higher maternal employment rates, national anti-poverty initiatives, and research showing the link between early childhood experiences and the brain development of young children. These factors have caused the rate of attendance in preschool programs to grow each year.

When Barrie's three children were preschool age in the 1990s and early 2000s, they all went to preschool, beginning at age three. In addition, they had enrichment activities after preschool, including music lessons, dance, and sports.

The parenting mindset at the time was to expose young children to a variety of enrichment programs (in addition to preschool) to give them a head start in kindergarten and hopefully foster

---

63 https://www.k12academics.com/systems-formal-education/preschool-educ ation/history-preschool-united-states

a passion or interest they could master prior to the college admissions process. This mindset is still alive and kicking today.

The intentions behind all of this scheduled activity for pre-schoolers is positive. Providing optimal learning environments that give children an academic leg up and set them up for future success is not a bad thing. But the unforeseen consequences of *overscheduling* hasn't served children or parents well.

Families are spending less quality time together, while their energy (and money) are being depleted. Both parents and kids feel overwhelmed, stressed-out, and pulled in too many directions without enough downtime or white space in between one activity and the next.

Parents are forced to rush their children in order to cram it all in, creating an environment of tension and anxiety—and sometimes anger—that's contagious and absorbed by young psyches who don't understand why piano lessons are so urgent.

In addition, there's immense pressure for parents to provide every opportunity for their children to get ahead—even children as young as preschoolers. The pressure comes not only from the parents' own dreams and goals for their children, but also from other parents who keep their children busy and scheduled in hopes of creating the next Michael Phelps or Simone Biles.

The messages parents are getting about overscheduling children are conflicting and confusing. On one hand, parents recognize all of this busyness isn't healthy. On the other, they don't want to risk letting their children miss out. And, truth be told, these activities provide another form of childcare that affords Mom and Dad a little more time to themselves.

Says author Bruce Feiler in an article[64] for the *New York Times*, "To absorb the conventional wisdom in parenting circles these days, what we're doing to our children is cruel, overbearing, and destructive to their long-term well-being. For years now, a consensus has been emerging that a subset of hard-driving, Ivy-longing parents is burdening their children with too many soccer tournaments, violin lessons, and cooking classes."

However, Feiler goes on to talk about the more recent backlash (based on research) to this belief, suggesting that afterschool enrichment programs and extracurricular activities are beneficial for children and can lead to more success in school and life.

And it's true—these programs are beneficial, as long as there's a balance between preschool, extracurricular activities, family life, and downtime. And as long as your preschooler is enjoying the activities and not feeling pressured by you to meet some expectation of performance.

It's hard to cultivate an atmosphere of mindfulness, peace, and gratitude in your home when your kids are being rushed through life. As a mindful parent, you'll need to choose the right balance of activities for your preschooler with discernment and care.

Let's go over some ways you can create balance in your child's life and what you need to consider in your thought processes.

Understand your child's personality.

Is your child more of an introvert who prefers time alone or with one or two friends? Or is he more extraverted and enjoys a lot of stimulation and activity? Is he more creative and intuitive,

---

64   https://www.nytimes.com/2013/10/13/fashion/over-scheduled-children
-how-big-a-problem.html

or logical and practical? Does he seem more athletic? Musical? Artistic?

By understanding your child's natural inclinations and interests, you can better discern the types and number of activities that will be best for him. Help guide him to a successful and positive experience when it comes to an extracurricular activity you're going to invest time and money into.

If your preschooler wants to participate in an activity that isn't suited to his personality, try to steer him to something that's a better fit.

Preschoolers aren't old enough to weigh the pros and cons of a decision, and they don't know themselves well enough to choose activities that aren't diametrically opposed to their personalities.

Honor your child's enthusiasm.

Your child might be swayed by peers, books, or movies to try a certain activity, revealing a budding interest in something. If you feel this interest is a fit with her personality, and you can find a program that supports your child's nature, then try to honor her enthusiasm.

Before you sign up for a program, ask if you can take your child for an observation class or if you can pay for a single lesson before you commit to a weekly activity. This trial run will save you from power struggles later on if your child changes her mind but you've already paid or made a commitment to a team or teacher.

One exception to honoring your child's interests should be swimming lessons. All children (whether or not they are interested in swimming) should have these lessons for their safety. The American Academy of Pediatrics recommends swimming lessons for all children age four or older.

Be realistic about your existing schedule and finances.

Before you sign up for an activity for your child, take a realistic look at your existing schedule.

- Does your child go to preschool? If so, how often?
- Is he enrolled in other activities?
- Is he involved in playgroups, or does he have regular playdates away from home?
- Do you have other children who have activities that require your time?
- Will the activity interfere with your work schedule, planned family time, or dinner hour?
- Do you have other adult commitments that should take precedence over extracurriculars for your child?

Be sure you have enough downtime both for your child and yourself, as well as plenty of time to spend together as a family. Rarely is any activity worth the sacrifice of enough free play and family time for your child.

Also, be sure that you're not stretching yourself financially to enroll a three- or four-year-old in an activity he will likely not remember down the road or may not stick with after a few weeks.

Look at your own motivations.

Think carefully about why you are enrolling your child in an activity. Is it because you feel pressured to do what other parents are doing? Are you hoping to mold a child prodigy? Do you think it will make her smarter or more competitive once she's in school?

For preschoolers, your main motivation should relate to your child's happiness, enjoyment, and well-being. Your child will have plenty of time to learn Spanish or master the violin when she's a little older. However, if she enjoys Spanish or violin lessons, and she still has plenty of time for free play, then give her the opportunity if you can afford it.

Before you enroll your child in any program, take a few minutes to examine your motivations and make sure they are serving your child rather than your own ego or insecurities. Allow your child to enjoy being a child as long as possible before she becomes immersed in the stress of achievement and competition.

Consider what your child is already getting in preschool.

If your child is enrolled in a preschool program, she may already be exposed to many of the activities you're considering. Most preschool programs include lessons in music, art, physical development, and technology.

Your child's preschool teacher can let you know if your child shows a particular interest or talent in an activity that you can explore further with an enrichment program when she's older. For now, the exposure in preschool may be enough to keep your little one engaged without feeling pressured or overscheduled.

Pay attention to stress levels and resistance.

Hopefully, your preschooler can't wait to go to soccer practice or piano lessons and hops in the car without you having to cajole her. But if you're consistently having to drag your child to an activity because she's too tired or disinterested, it's time to reconsider the activity.

Older children need to learn the importance of following through on a commitment to a team or to an activity they initially begged to join and that you paid good money for. But preschoolers don't have the ability to understand the potential consequences of a decision related to an extracurricular activity.

Young children are mercurial and change their minds often about what they find fascinating and fun. Sometimes the reality of what's involved in an activity doesn't match your child's notion of what it might be like. If your child is getting teary on the soccer field or whining that she hates piano lessons, let her stop the activity without guilt or anger (for your child or yourself).

Consider one activity at a time.

There are so many possibilities for enrichment programs for your child that it can be hard to decide what to choose. Often, parents select activities based on what they are interested in or what they want their children to excel in. Sometimes well-intentioned parents want to cover all the bases and enroll their children in multiple activities, with something going on every day.

If you have several children in various activities, your preschooler may be spending hours in the car waiting for siblings in addition to attending her own programs. This means there's little time for relaxation and free play at home because you're constantly rushing from one thing to the next.

For young preschoolers, consider offering just one enrichment activity a week (in addition to preschool), and allow that activity to be something your child really wants to do.

Consider delaying activities altogether.

If you decide to forgo extracurriculars altogether during the preschool years, your child won't be the worse for it. There will be plenty of time for your child to get involved in sports, music lessons, dance, or whatever he is interested in.

You can still expose your child to these activities without enrolling him in a formal program. You and your child can kick the soccer ball around in the yard or put on music and dance around the family room. You can play Spanish language cartoons or audio lessons, or get a small keyboard and teach your child music notes.

26. Simplify Your Child's Environment

If you enter the home of any family with small children, you're likely to find a play room or family room laden with plastic toys, games, blocks, play houses, dolls, figurines, and other blinking, flashing gizmos that are the latest and greatest temptations for kids. The child's bedroom is so cluttered with stuff that it looks more like a crazy fun house than a soothing place for sleep.

Parents may try to keep all of these items contained in bins and baskets, but every day toys are strewn across the floor and quickly abandoned. It's stressful for kids and parents alike to keep up with all of the stuff and maintain it in some semblance of order, especially when more toys keep coming in the door.

It's not just kids who long for material things and then quickly tire of them. In our consumer-oriented culture, adults are also addicted to stuff in order to satisfy the fleeting thrill of acquiring something new and shiny. But as adults, it's up to us to recognize the unhealthiness of this addiction—how it's cluttering our homes (and our psyches) and creating unnecessary anxiety for everyone in the family.

When your child frequently begs for new toys, it shows he's falling into a materialism vortex where the longing for something new is never satisfied. As an intentional parent, take this signal as an opportunity to reevaluate your philosophy related to toys and stuff in your home.

The truth is, preschoolers don't need that many toys—for their entertainment or their education. Children definitely need *play* for their development, but they don't necessarily need toys in order to play. In fact, your home is filled with normal household objects that can keep them well entertained without you having to purchase many toys.

A recent study[65] found that too many toys reduced the quality of play for children. When kids had fewer toys, they played with each toy longer, allowing them better focus to explore and play more creatively.

Two public health workers (Strick and Schubert) conducted an experiment[66] in which a German kindergarten classroom teacher removed all of the toys from the classroom for three months. During the initial stages of the experiment, the children were bored, but soon they began to use their basic surroundings to come up with games that involved imaginative play.

The researchers suggested that removing the toys helped children learn important social and life skills such as empathy, creativity, critical thinking, and the ability to resolve problems.

When there are dozens of toys crammed in a bin or cluttering a room, your child feels overwhelmed and agitated with so many choices. He may get bored or distracted and quickly become disinterested in any of them. So he begs for something new to stifle the boredom.

Couple the toy chaos with any general clutter and disorganization in your home and you're creating an environment that can cause your child stress and create problems with his emotional regulation. It can also impact his ability to focus and be present with any activity.

---

65   https://www.sciencedirect.com/science/article/abs/pii/S016363831730
1613
66   http://www.spielzeugfreierkindergarten.de/pdf/englisch.pdf

In our book *Declutter Your Mind*,[67] we discuss why clutter has such a negative impact on everyone in the home:

> Your home should be a haven—a place where you feel peaceful, happy, and calm. But can you feel this way when your home is cluttered with stuff?
>
> Researchers at the Princeton University Neuroscience Institute published the results of a study they conducted in *The Journal of Neuroscience* that relates directly to uncluttered and organized living. According to their report, "Interactions of Top-Down and Bottom-Up Mechanisms in Human Visual Cortex":
>
> *Multiple stimuli present in the visual field at the same time compete for neural representation by mutually suppressing their evoked activity throughout visual cortex, providing a neural correlate for the limited processing capacity of the visual system.*
>
> In other words, when your environment is cluttered, the visual chaos restricts your ability to focus. The clutter also limits your brain's ability to process information. Clutter distracts you so you're unable to process information as well as you would in an uncluttered, organized, and serene environment.

Fewer toys for your child means he will have more time for socialization with family and friends. Your child will become more resourceful and creative in his play and will focus more on mindful activities like coloring, painting, music, books, and outdoor play.

---

67 https://www.amazon.com/Declutter-Your-Mind-Eliminate-Mindfulness
-ebook/dp/B01KU04K5A

Also, when your child doesn't get every material thing he desires, he learns to value what he has, becomes less selfish, and feels more gratitude.

It may seem you're fighting a losing battle against all of the stuff accumulating in your home. With every holiday and birthday, more toys junk up your living spaces and are soon abandoned.

Every television commercial or pop-up ad on your devices entices your child to ask for just one more toy. And maybe you feel guilty saying no because you don't want to deprive your child of something he longs for (or seems to in the moment).

As a busy adult, you're already struggling to keep your home in some semblance of order, but with children in the house it can be overwhelming. How can you simplify and declutter your home to create an environment that reflects your commitment to mindfulness, simplicity, and peace? How can you teach your child that he doesn't need everything he wants? Let's go over some ideas that might inspire you.

Discuss your simplicity values with your child.

Talk with your child about why you value decluttering and simplifying your home and possessions. Let her know the benefits of having fewer toys (as outlined above) and focusing on those that spark creativity and engagement. Teach your child that possessions don't equal sustained happiness and that real joy is found in experiences and relationships.

You may need to let your older preschooler know that you have different values from some of her friends' families. She'll wonder why her friends have an abundance of toys but she's limited to a few. You'll feel the pressure to "keep up with the Joneses" and buy more toys, but mindful parenting sometimes involves sticking to your guns, even when it's uncomfortable.

These concepts are difficult for a preschooler to fully understand, but you're setting the stage for a mindset that will serve your child forever. Embracing the value that living with less provides more happiness in the long run will foster a more intentional, mindful, creative, and emotionally intelligent older child and adult.

Choose toys and games mindfully.

When you do purchase toys and games for your child, focus on quality over quantity—both in design and purpose. Choose toys that are well-made and that provide room for your child's imagination to enjoy them in a variety of ways.

Notice the toys and games your preschooler gravitates toward in stores or at friends' homes, and try to purchase those that suit your child's interests rather than his whims.

Resist the temptation to purchase toys you believe your child *should* play with, those that are the latest craze or those you hope will provide an "educational experience." You don't need to feel pressured to buy learning toys—your child is always learning through play and imagination.

Deborah MacNamara, a clinical counselor in Vancouver, and author of *Rest, Play, Grow: Making Sense of Preschoolers*, suggests in an article in Today's Parent[68] that kids need the freedom to choose their own experiences with toys and play:

> To allow for individual expression from a child onto their environment, it is preferable to have open-ended things like blocks, blank canvases, and things that do not press onto a child a certain outcome. Play is no longer play when adults impose outcomes on what things should look like or determine how they should function.

Toy fads come and go, but few stand the test of time by inspiring your child to play and think creatively. Consider prioritizing the following toys—some of which have been around for decades:

- Legos
- Wooden blocks and bricks
- Lincoln Logs
- Tinker Toys
- Plastic animals and dinosaurs
- Matchbox cars
- Playmobil
- Puzzles
- Marble runs
- Art supplies
- Musical instruments
- Play kitchen and play foods
- Doll house, wooden dolls
- Toy workbench

68 https://www.todaysparent.com/family/parenting/how-many-toys-do-kids -really-need/

- Fisher Price Little People
- Wooden train set
- Board games
- Dress-up clothes
- Play-Doh
- Doctor's kit
- Balls
- Dump trucks
- Water table
- Sandbox
- Tricycle, bicycle, scooter

Practice the twenty-toy rule.

How many toys does your child really need? If you ask the German researchers mentioned previously, she doesn't need any toys at all. Having no toys might make your child more creative and resourceful, but for most parents, the idea is a bit extreme.

So how many toys is the right number? There's no hard and fast rule, but we suggest you use the "twenty-toy rule" as a guide. At any one time, your child has a selection of only twenty toys she can choose from. Here's how it works.

- Ask your preschooler to select twenty toys that are her favorite, or that "spark joy," as decluttering guru Marie Kondo[69] suggests. Try to guide her to choose some that are open-ended and require creativity and focus.

---

69   https://konmari.com

- From the remaining toys, purge any that are broken or that your child no longer plays with. Throw away the broken toys and donate the others.

- Put the toys that remain in storage containers and label what's inside of each box. Put the boxes out of sight so your child can't easily pull them out.

- When your child gets tired of the existing toys, tell him he can "check out" another toy from your toy library (toys in storage), as long as he turns in a toy and puts it in the storage box. He can switch out as many toys as he likes, but he must keep the total to twenty toys.

- If a new toy comes into the house, he must store or donate one of his twenty. When you donate toys, talk to your pre-schooler about the value of giving to others. You can take your preschooler on an outing to a medical center, nonprofit organization, local church, homeless shelter, orphanage, school, or Goodwill to give them away. If you store a lot of toys and find the storage boxes are accumulating, you may need to purge again to get rid of toys that never get used.

You may want to make some exceptions to your twenty-toy rule. For example, a collection of stuffed animals, dolls, or soldiers (and accessories) might count as one toy. Or you might not count family games as part of the twenty your child selects. You may have sentimental toys that are gifts from family members that you want to display rather than tossing in a storage box.

You can set the rules for how you limit the number of toys. The goal is simply to limit them and maintain that limit so your child's need for stuff isn't so overwhelming. If he knows he has a limit, he will beg for toys less and be more discerning about the toys he asks for. Just remember—fewer toys doesn't mean more TV and tech time.

Keep toys and supplies your child selects easily accessible and organized so he will be encouraged to play with them. Have a place for everything, and teach your child to put things back once he's finished playing. You can find hundreds of creative toy organization ideas on Pinterest by typing "toy organization ideas" in the search bar.

Don't give into begging or tantrums at stores.

One of the most difficult places to maintain your resolve about toys is when you are out shopping with your child in tow. Grocery stores, convenience stores, Walmart, Target, and department stores are filled with tempting eye candy for your child.

You can make a preemptive strike by telling your preschooler before you walk in the door that you are not purchasing any toys. But even if your child knows your rules about toys, she's still going to ask for something. That's what children do. How you respond to the ask and to the resulting reaction is paramount in teaching your child about your values and your resolve.

Hopefully, all it will take is you stating in a firm voice, "I already told you that we were not buying any toys. Please don't ask me again." But if your child keeps begging or has a meltdown when you say no, you'll need to take swift action and leave the store.

Even if you have a cart full of groceries, you may need to abandon it to show your preschooler that you mean what you say. Tell her that you're leaving the store because she didn't listen when you said no toys. You don't need to get angry—just show her you mean business.

It's a daunting prospect when you have little time for errands and you need the groceries (or whatever you're shopping for). But if you give in and buy the toy just to stop the begging or crying, you're showing your child she can get what she wants by acting out in public.

If you absolutely can't leave the store, take your child (and your shopping cart) aside to a restroom or out-of-the-way area until she calms down. Later, let her know that she won't be able to go to the store with you the next time—a natural consequence for her behavior.

If you decide on occasion that you want to reward your child with a purchase or buy her a toy just because, be sure to explain why you are making an exception. Try not to make these exceptions when your child is begging or acting out.

Give your child a small allowance.

You can manage the potential toy begging issue (and teach your child the value of money at the same time) by giving him a small allowance. The allowance can be tied to chores, or you may want to freely give a small weekly amount of money and require him to save part of it.

Either way, let your preschooler know that if he wants something at the store, he'll need to use his allowance to buy it. Then, if he asks for a toy, you can say, "Yes! You can buy it with your allowance." This frees you from the stress of constantly saying no to repeated requests.

If your child doesn't have enough money for what he wants, let him know that you have to make similar difficult decisions when it comes to making purchases. Talk with him about saving his allowance for the toy, or for something he likes better. He will learn to prioritize his purchases and choose carefully.

Discuss your toy philosophy with extended family.

Grandparents, aunts and uncles, and other relatives may not share your more minimalist philosophy about toys for your child. In fact, they may take great pleasure in purchasing toys for birthdays and holidays, or any time they visit your child.

You don't want to squash their joy in gift-giving, but if grand-parents and others are open to a conversation about it, share your mindfulness values about toys for your preschooler. Talk with relatives about gifting your child with experiences rather than things. Or suggest gifts from the previous list of toys that are more open-ended and creative.

When new toys come into the house as gifts, remember to have your child select an equal number of toys to put in the storage box or give away.

Be a "less is more" role model.

The best way to reinforce your values about simplifying and living with less stuff is by being a role model to your child. If you're asking your preschooler to minimize her toys and keep them organized and put away, you need to be equally mindful about your own stuff. If your shelves, cabinets, and closets are overflowing and you frequently come home with new purchases, you're giving your child a mixed message.

Ask your preschooler to help you purge some of your things so she can see you practicing what you preach. Talk about how someone else can use the clothes, books, and household items that you are letting go. Make simplifying and decluttering a family affair so that it becomes increasingly clear that "things" are not the priority in your family.

If you want more ideas on decluttering and minimizing stuff, check out the books *10-Minute Declutter: The Stress-Free Habit for Simplifying Your Home*[70] by Steve Scott and Barrie Davenport and *Clutterfree with Kids: Change Your Thinking, Discover New Habits, Free Your Home*[71] by Joshua Becker.

---

70   https://www.amazon.com/10-Minute-Declutter-Stress-Free-Habit-Simpl ifying-ebook/dp/B00XQGSPES

71   https://www.amazon.com/Clutterfree-Kids-thinking-Discover-habits-ebo ok/dp/B00HYNJKCU

Final Thoughts on Mindful Parenting Habits

We'd like to start this final section by *thanking you*. By reading this book all the way to the end, you've demonstrated a commitment to live more in the present moment with your child. Sure, caring for a little one can be stressful, but you've taken that crucial first step toward making a positive change.

As we stated before, practicing mindful parenting gives you the mental focus to be proactive rather than reactive, and to be thoughtful in your interactions with your children, your spouse, and yourself. It helps you navigate the challenges you'll face with your child *without* saying something you later regret. And it helps you maintain a close connection with your child.

Simply put: Practicing mindful parenting can have many positive effects on you and your child.

Now, before we close things out, we strongly recommend that you implement what you've learned. While it would be impossible to implement all twenty-six practices that we've covered, we recommend **starting with one mindful habit** that you can incorporate into your daily routine.

If you feel stuck with *where* to focus your efforts, then we recommend a simple strategy:

Examine your current parenting situation and focus on the one area where you need the most help.

If you have an infant and you're struggling with the challenges of chaotic feeding schedules, or a lack of sleep, then we recommend picking one of the strategies that help you stay in the moment without feeling stressed. Like practicing present moment awareness, expressing gratitude for the limited time you have with your baby, or using the Three Mindful Breaths technique whenever you feel stressed out.

If you're dealing with a challenging toddler who has frequent tantrums, then we recommend a couple of the strategies. Like using the STOP Method to immediately deal with your toddler's meltdown or creating a predictable routine that can curb many future tantrums.

And if your child is a preschooler, then this will be the perfect time to share the gift of mindfulness with him. One strategy that works is to turn mindfulness into a game that is both fun and educational. Alternatively, if your preschooler still struggles with controlling his feelings, you can practice active listening to help him sort out those challenging emotions.

It doesn't matter how old your child is, you can find *at least* one idea in this book to incorporate more mindfulness into your parenting style. The hard part is getting started. That's why we urge you to immediately review the twenty-six habits that we've covered, pick one that sounds interesting, and try it today!

Finally, remember that this time with your child is fleeting. While you might feel stressed and overwhelmed right now, you are also experiencing moments that will become cherished memories down the road. The trick is to take the time to pause and savor these little experiences. And hopefully this book has helped you do just that.

We wish you the best of luck!

Barrie Davenport & S.J. Scott

More Books by Steve

The Anti-Procrastination Habit: A Simple Guide to Mastering Difficult Tasks

10-Minute Mindfulness: 71 Habits for Living in the Present Moment

Habit Stacking: 127 Small Actions to Improve Your Health, Wealth, and Happiness

Novice to Expert: 6 Steps to Learn Anything, Increase Your Knowledge, and Master New Skills

Declutter Your Mind: How to Stop Worrying, Relieve Anxiety, and Eliminate Negative Thinking

The Miracle Morning for Writers: How to Build a Writing Ritual That Increases Your Impact and Your Income

10-Minute Digital Declutter: The Simple Habit to Eliminate Technology Overload

10-Minute Declutter: The Stress-Free Habit for Simplifying Your Home

The Accountability Manifesto: How Accountability Helps You Stick to Goals

Confident You: An Introvert's Guide to Success in Life and Business

Exercise Every Day: 32 Tactics for Building the Exercise Habit (Even If You Hate Working Out)

The Daily Entrepreneur: 33 Success Habits for Small Business Owners, Freelancers and Aspiring 9-to-5 Escape Artists

Master Evernote: The Unofficial Guide to Organizing Your Life with Evernote (Plus 75 Ideas for Getting Started)

Bad Habits No More: 25 Steps to Break Any Bad Habit

Habit Stacking: 97 Small Life Changes That Take Five Minutes or Less

To-Do List Makeover: A Simple Guide to Getting the Important Things Done

23 Anti-Procrastination Habits: Overcome Your Procrastination and Get Results in Your Life

S.M.A.R.T. Goals Made Simple: 10 Steps to Master Your Personal and Career Goals

115 Productivity Apps to Maximize Your Time: Apps for iPhone, iPad, Android, Kindle Fire and PC/iOS Desktop Computers

Writing Habit Mastery: How to Write 2,000 Words a Day and Forever Cure Writer's Block

Daily Inbox Zero: 9 Proven Steps to Eliminate Email Overload

Wake Up Successful: How to Increase Your Energy and Achieve Any Goal with a Morning Routine

10,000 Steps Blueprint: The Daily Walking Habit for Healthy Weight Loss and Lifelong Fitness

70 Healthy Habits: How to Eat Better, Feel Great, Get More Energy and Live a Healthy Lifestyle

Resolutions That Stick! How 12 Habits Can Transform Your New Year

More Books by Barrie

Declutter Your Mind: How to Stop Worrying, Relieve Anxiety, and Eliminate Negative Thinking

10-Minute Digital Declutter: The Simple Habit to Eliminate Technology Overload

10-Minute Declutter: The Stress-Free Habit for Simplifying Your Home

201 Relationship Questions: The Couple's Guide to Building Trust and Emotional Intimacy

Self-Discovery Questions: 155 Breakthrough Questions to Accelerate Massive Action

Sticky Habits: 6 Simple Steps to Create Good Habits That Stick

Finely Tuned: How To Thrive As A Highly Sensitive Person or Empath

Peace of Mindfulness: Everyday Rituals to Conquer Anxiety and Claim Unlimited Inner Peace

Confidence Hacks: 99 Small Actions to Massively Boost Your Confidence

Building Confidence: Get Motivated, Overcome Social Fear, Be Assertive, and Empower Your Life for Success

The 52-Week Life Passion Project: The Path to Uncover Your Life Passion

Made in the USA
Middletown, DE
21 January 2020